WITHDRAWN

Alexander Pope

Epistles to Several Persons
(MORAL ESSAYS)

Introduction and Notes

by

JAMES E. WELLINGTON

UNIVERSITY OF MIAMI

CARL A. RUDISILL LIBRARY
LENOIR RHYNE COLLEGE

821.5
P81e

Copyright 1963

by

James E. Wellington

Library of Congress Number 63-21348

UNIVERSITY OF MIAMI
CRITICAL STUDIES

UNIVERSITY OF MIAMI PRESS
CORAL GABLES, FLORIDA

Printed in the United States of America

by

Atlantic Printers and Lithographers, Inc.

Miami Beach, Florida

ACKNOWLEDGMENTS

The author wishes to acknowledge with gratitude the kindness of the following publishers in permitting brief quotations from books on which they hold copyright:

George Allen & Unwin Ltd., 40 Museum Street, London W.C.1, England

Doubleday & Company, Inc., 575 Madison Avenue, New York 22, New York (Anchor Books)

Harcourt, Brace & World, Inc., 757 Third Avenue, New York 17, New York

Harper and Row, Publishers, Inc., 49 East 33rd Street, New York 16, New York

Harvard University Press, 79 Garden Street, Cambridge 38, Massachusetts

The Johns Hopkins Press, Baltimore 18, Maryland

Methuen & Co., Ltd., 30 Essex Street, Strand, London W.C.2, England

Oxford University Press, Inc., 417 Fifth Avenue, New York 16, New York

The Viking Press, Inc., 625 Madison Avenue, New York 22, New York

Yale University Press, 92A Yale Station, New Haven, Connecticut

Bibliographical Note

Printed in William Warburton's 1751 edition of Pope's works is an Advertisement to the Moral Essays describing a grand philosophical project in which the four poems and the *Essay on Man* were to play an important part.[1] This was to have been a "Greater Essay on Man" in four books, a thorough examination of human nature in the light of ethical responsibilities, social relationships, and intellectual accomplishments and ambitions. The *Essay on Man* as it now stands was to have formed the first book; the second and third books were never written; the Moral Essays were to have been included in Book IV, although in the editions of 1735 and 1736 they were published as *Ethic Epistles, the Second Book*. Pope's letters indicate that the project significantly occupied his thoughts in the early 1730's,[2] but the Advertisement declares that for various reasons its completion began to seem a rather heavy chore, and the idea was gradually abandoned. From *Ethic Epistles* the title was accordingly changed to the more neutral *Epistles to Several Persons* for the editions of 1739 and 1743 (Griffith 505, 583);[3] the title *Moral Essays*, apparently Warburton's innovation for the edition of 1751,[4] never appeared in Pope's lifetime.

The role which the four epistles were intended to play in this ambitious semi-Horatian enterprise helps to account for

1 *The Works of Alexander Pope*, ed. William Warburton, 9 vols. (London: J. and P. Knapton, 1751), III, 163-165 (hereinafter cited as *Warburton*).

2 Cf. Pope to Swift, November 28, 1729 (last sentence), and January 6, 1734 (N.S.), in which he refers to his *Opus Magnum*; *The Correspondence of Alexander Pope*, ed. George Sherburn, 5 vols. (Oxford: The Clarendon Press, 1956), III, 81, 401, (hereinafter cited as *Corr.*).

3 Reginald Harvey Griffith, *Alexander Pope: A Bibliography*, 2 vols. (Austin: University of Texas Press, 1927); the numbers cited are item numbers in Griffith's bibliography.

4 Warburton was also responsible for calling the *Epistle to Arbuthnot* the "Prologue to the Satires," and the two dialogues of 1738 the "Epilogue to the Satires."

the thematic relationship which they bear to one another and to the *Essay on Man*. These relationships are discussed in some detail in the commentaries which follow. In general, Pope is concerned throughout the four poems with a number of his favorite subjects—the irrational extremes of human behavior, and God's way of bringing ultimate good out of them; the Golden Mean between the extremes; the Ruling Passion as a motive for action, and the role of reason in directing it; and the desirability of looking at the world, for all its individual tragedy and injustice, as a fundamentally good place, created by a loving and benevolent God, in which the general welfare is paramount and will in the long run be served. Epistles I and II (the third and fourth, respectively, to be published) emphasize irrational and puzzling inconsistencies in human nature itself, and in Epistle I the Ruling Passion receives its fullest treatment since the second epistle of the *Essay on Man*. Epistles III and IV (the second and first, respectively, in order of original publication) are concerned with extremes and abuses in the handling of money, with emphasis on such matters as avarice, profusion, and charity (Epistle III), and tasteless ostentation and true splendor (Epistle IV). These are all ideas which appear prominently in much of Pope's other poetry, as do many of the people whom Pope attacks or praises in the Moral Essays.

At the same time, however, it would be inaccurate to describe these four epistles as essentially didactic poetry in the spirit of the *Essay on Man*. Whatever may have been their intended function in what seems, on the whole, to have been a didactic scheme, the epistles are in reality something rather different from the "moral essays" which Warburton imagined them to be. Pope's discourse in these poems is in part ethical and philosophical, to be sure, but the spirit of satire is nevertheless dominant, whereas in the *Essay on Man* just the reverse is true. Pope is seldom doing exclusively one thing or the other, and he often uses satire for ethical and

2

philosophical purposes; the *Epistle to Bathurst*, the most
didactic of the four poems, often becomes patently satirical,
whereas the *Epistle to a Lady*, surely the most satirical of the
four, has perceptible elements of didacticism as well. From
the standpoint of thematic emphasis and emotional tone, the
Epistles to Several Persons occupy a position somewhere between the *Essay on Man*, on the one hand, and the *Imitations
of Horace* and *The Dunciad* on the other; and they betray
numerous echoes—or anticipations, as the case may be—of
all these poems. Many of these parallels are considered in the
commentaries and notes of the present volume.

Pope's *Epistles to Several Persons* (this was, after all,
Pope's personal and final choice for a title) have undergone
some rather curious vicissitudes of emendation and change,
notably at the hands of Warburton. Pope met Warburton
relatively late in life—the year was 1740, to be exact—but
the two men were enormously impressed with each other.
Warburton, in fact, had already performed a notable service
for Pope. The *Essay on Man*, published anonymously in 1733
and 1734, had received great acclaim in England and was popularly thought to have been the work of a divine. In 1737,
however, it had come under attack, on the grounds of fatalism
and necessitarianism, from an unexpected quarter, the Swiss
Calvinist theologian Jean Pierre de Crousaz (1663-1750).
Warburton, himself a prominent Anglican churchman, sprang
immediately to Pope's defense, and Pope was grateful.[5] When
the two men finally came face to face, therefore, the friendship prospered; and Pope subsequently named Warburton his
literary executor, an appointment which later generations have
had occasion to regret.

Thus armed with the poet's confidence and the legal rights
to his work, Warburton busied himself with the task of assist-

---

5 The title of Crousaz's work was *Examen de l'essai de M. Pope sur
l'homme* (1737).

ing Pope in the preparation of a last great edition of Pope's poems, an edition which Pope himself, who in 1743 felt his life drawing to a close, earnestly hoped would stand as his final testament to the world. When the poet died, on May 30, 1744, the edition was still incomplete for all his labors, but the *Epistles to Several Persons* (as they were then entitled) had been printed with Pope's final emendations. This printing, the so-called "deathbed" edition of the epistles, was suppressed, probably to mollify the Duchess of Marlborough, who fancied that the poems contained unpleasant allusions to herself and the late Duke—although the British Museum volume which forms the basis of the Twickenham Edition text is probably a surviving copy.[6] In the pursuit of his duties as editor, Warburton took a number of very great liberties with the texts of *To Cobham* and *To Bathurst*. Dissatisfied with the organization of the *Epistle to Cobham*, he drastically rearranged the poem, transposing lines and passages from one place to another to suit his personal conception of the logical structure of the poem. The sheer effrontery of Warburton's own statement to this effect has to be read to be believed:

> Whoever compares this with the former Editions of this poem [i.e., *To Cobham*], will observe that the order and disposition of the several parts are entirely changed and transposed, tho' with hardly the Alteration of a single word. When the Editor, at the Author's desire, first examined this Epistle, he was surprised to find it contain a number of fine observations, without order, connexion, or dependence: but much more so, when, on an attentive review, he saw, that, if put into a different form, on an idea he then conceived, it would have all the clearness of method, and force of connected reasoning. Indeed the observations then appeared to him so jumbled and con-

---

6 *The Twickenham Edition of the Poems of Alexander Pope*, gen. ed. John Butt, 6 vols. (London: Methuen and Co., Ltd., 1939-1954), Vol. III, Part ii, *Epistles to Several Persons* (*Moral Essays*), ed. F. W. Bateson, p. xv (hereinafter cited as TE).

founded in one another, as if the several parts of a regular poem had been rolled up in tickets, drawn at random, and then set down as they arose. The author appeared as much struck with the observation as the editor, and agreed to put it in the present form, which has given the poem all the justness of a true composition. The introduction of the epistle on Riches [i.e., *To Bathurst*] was in the same condition and underwent the same reform.[7]

And so it did, for Warburton changed the *Epistle to Bathurst* into a dialogue between Pope and Bathurst, merely by placing *P* in front of some lines and *B* in front of a few others, in addition to a similar tampering with the organization of the poem. All this was accomplished, as Warburton says, with no alteration in the wording of the poems as Pope had emended them before his death, for Pope's will expressly forbade such changes.

How much Pope knew of all this is a difficult question. Warburton, of course, says that he acquiesced, but Warburton's statements about Pope and his works are sometimes disingenuous and untrustworthy. If Pope did agree to the changes, the likelihood is that in 1744 he was too ill or too busy or too much in awe of Warburton's supposed critical abilities to offer any serious protest. At all events, Warburton's transpositions have done more harm than good. They have rendered *To Cobham* in many respects illogical; and, as Samuel Johnson observed, to change what was originally an epistle to Lord Bathurst into a dialogue between the poet and Bathurst seems quite pointless—especially since Bathurst is given so little to say and since the device effects a complete exchange of character between the two speakers, in the "dialogue" beginning at line 21.[8]

Warburton's mischief, moreover, has perpetuated itself

---

7 Warburton, 163
8 Cf. TE, 5-11.

over the years. These alterations, which first appeared in the "deathbed" edition of 1744, Warburton incorporated into his 1751 edition of Pope's works, along with his new title for the four poems; and all subsequent editors save one have followed him blindly, although Courthope voiced disapproval of the changes while retaining them.[9] This state of affairs continued for exactly two centuries, when, in 1951, the Twickenham Edition, now the definitive edition of Pope's poetry, restored the organization of *To Cobham* and *To Bathurst* which Pope himself had allowed to stand for a decade. For the present volume, the Dodsley and Cooper edition of 1743 (Griffith 583, printed as Appendix I in the Elwin-Courthope edition) has been used as a basic text for the epistles to Cobham and Bathurst. This has been collated with Warburton's edition of 1751, a procedure which effectually removes all traces of Warburton's tampering without sacrificing Pope's own emendations of 1744. The other two epistles (*To a Lady* and *To Burlington*) present few textual problems and are accordingly given here in the text of 1751. In a few quite obvious instances, erroneous punctuation in the 1751 edition has been silently corrected, usually to make it conform to the punctuation of 1743. Pope's own spellings, which are rarely so archaic as to be confusing, have been retained in the interests of authenticity; his capitalization, which is sometimes significant for his meaning, has also been preserved.

The publishing history of the *Epistles to Several Persons* from their first appearance as single poems to Warburton's edition of 1751 is somewhat complex. Each epistle was published separately, in folio, as soon as it was finished: *To Cobham* in January 1734 (dated 1733) (Griffith 329); *To a Lady* in February 1735 (Griffith 360); *To Bathurst* in January

---

9 *The Works of Alexander Pope*, ed. Whitwell Elwin and William John Courthope, 10 vols. (London: John Murray, 1871-1889), III, 49-51 (hereinafter cited as EC).

1733 (dated 1732) (Griffith 280-283); *To Burlington* in December 1731 (Griffith 259). *To Bathurst* went to a second edition in 1733 (Griffith 323, 324), and *To Burlington* appeared in a second and third edition in 1731 (Griffith 265, 267). All four were gathered together in 1735 in Vol. II of Pope's *Works* of that year, of which there were five editions. This volume reappeared, without noteworthy textual changes, in 1736, 1739, 1740, and 1743. In 1744 the suppressed "deathbed" edition, with many significant textual changes, was printed but never sold. Warburton's edition of 1751 is largely based upon this edition of 1744, and all subsequent editions, save for the Twickenham Edition of 1951, have been based on Warburton.[10]

---

10 This is a condensation of material supplied in TE's textual introduction to the four epistles.

EPISTLE I

To Sir Richard Temple, Lord Cobham

The *Epistle to Cobham*, like the other three Moral Essays, was originally published alone, as an individual poem, and appeared for the first time on January 16, 1734 (N. S.). The subtitle which it bore on that occasion was "Of the Knowledge and Characters of Men," a designation which only partially describes the theme of the poem. The *Epistle to Cobham* was actually the third of the Moral Essays in point of original publication, but when Pope gathered the four epistles together for the first time, for inclusion in the second volume of his *Works* (April 1735; Griffith 370), he adopted the order in which they have ever since been published: *To Cobham, To a Lady, To Bathurst, To Burlington.* The reason for this arrangement was doubtless the role the epistles were intended to play in the grand philosophical scheme outlined above. In this "Greater Essay on Man," as we have already seen, the *Essay on Man* in its present form was to have comprised the first book of the whole. The second book, also in four epistles, was to have dealt with problems arising from human reason, the arts, and the sciences, amplifying Epistles I and II of the *Essay.* The third was to have been a discussion of man in public life—politics, religion, and society—amplifying Epistle III of the *Essay.* Book four, which most directly concerns the present poem, would have pursued "the subject of the *Fourth* Epistle of the *First* [i.e., of the *Essay on Man*], and treats of *Ethics,* or practical Morality; and would have consisted of many members; of which the four following Epistles [i.e., the Moral Essays] were detached portions: the *two first,* on the *Characters of Men and Women* being the *introductory* part of this concluding Book."[11] Thus did the

---

11 Warburton, 165. Pope explained the design to Spence in retrospect shortly before his death; cf. Joseph Spence, *Anecdotes, Observations,*

Epistle to Cobham find its way from third to first position among the four Moral Essays.

The phrasing of this Advertisement raises a pertinent question concerning Pope's intentions with regard to the *Epistle to Cobham*. Does the subtitle, "Of the Knowledge and Characters of Men," refer to the male sex only, or does it mean all mankind? Since the epistle which follows bears the subtitle "Of the Characters of Women," the temptation immediately arises to choose the former interpretation and to regard the two epistles together as complementary, the first dealing with one sex, the second with the other. *To Cobham*, moreover, is addressed to a man and the characters are predominantly male, whereas *To a Lady* is addressed to Martha Blount, and the characters are exclusively female. Finally, there is the last paragraph of the Advertisement, which lumps these first two epistles together under the collective heading "Characters of Men and Women."

Now, the Advertisement of 1751, originally written in 1743 or 1744 for the "deathbed edition" of the Moral Essays, may have been written by Pope himself, or it may have been written by Warburton, who, as we have seen, was Pope's literary executor. The evidence is not conclusive either way; and, no matter who wrote the Advertisement, it would be helpful in determining what Pope thought of it to know exactly when it was composed and what the state of Pope's health was when the actual formulation took place. Pope knew that he was dying; and a man preparing what he conceives to be a deathbed edition of his own works may well be in too great a hurry to concern himself overmuch with small details of phraseology in an Advertisement. Such matters he will in all likelihood relinquish to a trusted and respected editor. In any case, the phrase "Characters of Men and

---

and Characters of Books and Men (London: W. H. Carpenter, 1820), p. 315 (hereinafter cited as Spence).

Women" may be nothing more than a conveniently shortened reference to two epistles which had already been published separately, as well as together, some years before and with which the reading public might be assumed to be tolerably familiar.

The fact that the *Epistle to Cobham* is addressed to a man and is largely about male characters is likewise inconclusive. The most elaborate portrait in the poem, to be sure, is that of the Duke of Wharton; and several other male characters are striking, through considerably shorter—Catius, Helluo, Euclio, and the rest. But there are also two portraits of women in the epistle. The first is that of "the frugal Crone" (lines 238-241), who spends her dying breath trying to blow out the candle; and this was added in 1744, when the Advertisement in question was also included. The second is that of the vain Narcissa, whose last words are instructions to her maid as to the manner in which her corpse shall be decked out for burial (lines 242-247); this passage is in the pre-1744 editions. Each of these two vignettes serves to illustrate the persistence of the Ruling Passion as the only stable element in human nature, and Pope makes it perfectly clear in both epistles that instability and the Ruling Passion alike are to be found throughout all human nature, regardless of sex. The Ruling Passion, furthermore, which receives extended treatment in the *Epistle to Cobham*, is at least adumbrated not only in the *Epistle to a Lady* but in the following two epistles as well. In short, there is good reason to suppose that Pope meant the *Epistle to Cobham* to be a discussion of human nature in general, not of the male sex in its essential masculinity, whereas the epistle following was to show more specifically the shifting vagaries of humanity in the female character. A brief glance at the Arguments of the two poems will serve to strengthen this belief still further, and Warburton's note to the first line of *To a Lady* is also helpful. It reads in part as follows:

11

But if [the reader] would reflect, that the *two Sexes* make but *one Species*, and consequently, that the Characters of both must be studied and explained on the same principles, he would see, that when the poet had done this in the preceding Epistle [i.e., *To Cobham*], his business here was, not to repeat what he had already delivered, but only to verify and illustrate his doctrine, by every *view* of that perplexity of Nature, which *his* philosophy only can explain. . . . [The reader] will see that the poet has all the while strictly followed Nature, whose ways, we find by the former Epistle [*To Cobham*], are not a little mysterious; and a mystery this might have remained, had not our author explained it at v. 207, ...[12]

This also helps to explain why *To a Lady* is the most patently satirical of the four epistles.

In the matter of human inconsistency, both Courthope and Bateson have called attention to the possible influence of Montaigne's essay "Of the inconsistency of our actions" (Book II, Chapter 1), an essay which Pope praised highly to Joseph Spence.[13] Here Montaigne despairs even more than Pope of ever being able to judge men's actions correctly, and there are one or two details in the *Epistle to Cobham* which parallel Montaigne's essay. There is some question, however, whether Montaigne (at least in this essay) goes so far as to admit the Ruling Passion as a reliable means of evaluating human nature and conduct. In the following passage it is not entirely clear whether he is referring to the Ruling Passion as Pope understood it; but if he is, he is surely discrediting it as a guide to character analysis:

There is some justification for basing a judgment of a man on the most ordinary acts of his life; but

---

12 Warburton, 194.

13 George Sherburn, "Pope at Work," *Essays on the Eighteenth Century Presented to David Nichol Smith* (Oxford: The Clarendon Press, 1945), p. 50 (hereinafter cited as "Pope at Work").

in view of the natural instability of our conduct and opinions, it has often seemed to me that even good authors are wrong to insist on fashioning a consistent and solid fabric out of us. They choose one general characteristic, and go and arrange and interpret all a man's actions to fit their picture, and if they cannot twist them enough, they go and set them down to dissimulation.[14]

Montaigne may be referring here to the theory of humours, but the theory of humours and the Ruling Passion have much in common. And then, at the end of the same paragraph, he says plainly that any attempt to judge character by general rule is doomed to failure:

Nothing is harder for me than to believe in men's consistency, nothing easier than to believe in their inconsistency. He who would judge them in detail, bit by bit, would more often hit upon the truth.[15]

This is a piecemeal manner of judging men which Pope deplores throughout the *Epistle to Cobham.*

On the other hand, in Montaigne's "The Story of Spurina" (Book II, Chapter 33), there may be, as Bateson suggests,[16] an anticipation of the Ruling Passion. At any rate, Montaigne here uses the example of Julius Caesar, just as Pope does (lines 210-221), to illustrate the distinction between primary and secondary motives. He shows—and Pope appears to follow him in this—that although Caesar may seem to be motivated by lust, lust is not really his Ruling Passion; he is merely using his amours as an occasional relief from the business of gratifying a more deeply rooted passion—ambition and the thirst for glory:

---

14 *The Complete Essays of Montaigne,* trans. Donald M. Frame, 3 vols. (Garden City, N.Y.: Doubleday and Co., Inc., 1960), II, 1-2 (hereinafter cited as Montaigne). Cf. *Ep. Cob.,* lines 71-76.

15 *Loc. cit.*

16 TE, 32.

> [Caesar was] a man extremely addicted to . . .
> debauch and of a very amorous constitution. But the
> other passion of ambition, coming into conflict with
> this one, promptly made it give way. . . . His pleasures
> never made him steal a single minute of time, or turn
> aside one step, from the occasions that presented
> themselves for his aggrandizement.[17]

Pope's discussion of Caesar sounds very much like this, and
it is well known from Spence that Pope read, enjoyed, and
admired Montaigne. It is also clear that Pope's skepticism
concerning the real nature of truth and its accessibility to
observation and reason is often close to the Pyrrhonism of
Montaigne, although it was not strong enough to turn him,
as it did Dryden, toward an increasingly authoritarian view
of church and state. But Pope's borrowings (if that is the
word) from Montaigne in the *Epistle to Cobham* are difficult to pinpoint specifically. Both men were obviously struck
with the incomprehensibility of human nature; but, for that
matter, so is everyone else, and the question of Montaigne's
influence on Pope, for which Spence is the chief authority,
had probably better be left at that.

From what has already been said, it should be apparent
that one of the basic themes of the *Epistle to Cobham* is the
inconsistency of human nature. From this inconsistency it
logically follows that human character is exceedingly difficult
to analyze; and the opening lines of the epistle, which are
disarmingly casual (Joseph Warton greatly disliked them),
contain the germ of a very important statement concerning
two possible ways of approaching the problem. These two
methods of character analysis represent, in typically neo-classic
fashion, two opposite extremes, neither of which, taken alone,
can be regarded by a rational man as adequate. The approach
to human nature ostensibly espoused by Cobham (as Pope
makes clear at the outset) is empirical and is predicated upon

---

17 Montaigne, II, 439-440.

the practical value of first-hand experience. Characteristically, its proponents feel little but contempt for the rationalist philosopher, the man of books, who tries to analyze human nature almost on an *a priori* basis from the confines of his library and his intellect. This, in rough outline, is a famous epistemological conflict with which the seventeenth and eighteenth centuries were well acquainted, from Descartes to Kant. Pope, however, is not a formal philosopher, and he steps in (at line 9) to reduce the argument to a pair of relatively simple extremes, between which can be clearly discerned a concept very close to Pope's heart, the Golden Mean. Neither the scholar nor the man of the world (Pope explains) has a monopoly of truth; neither, by exclusive reliance on his own methods, can hope to fathom the perplexities of his fellow man. The perceptions gained by first-hand experience are continually corrupted by passion, prejudice, or imagination (lines 23-28); and sensory impressions, furthermore, are too rapid and too fleeting for reliable observation (lines 29-34). An abstract understanding of basic principles, on the other hand, is similarly defeated because the very principles themselves are phantoms which shift and change with every passing moment (lines 35-40). Only by a judicious combination of both methods—that is, by striking a Golden Mean between them—can the observer hope to grasp the elusive inconsistencies of human nature.

This blend of observation and ratiocination—which in reality is little more than the inescapable mixture of inductive and deductive principles common in all logic—will eventually reveal the essence of a man's character, his Ruling Passion. But even here the observer must draw his conclusions warily, for there is still danger, as Caesar's character shows (lines 210-221), of mistaking appearance for reality, of mistaking for a true Ruling Passion a secondary trait which only looks like one. Nevertheless, it is the Ruling Passion, Pope is asking us to believe, which affords the only real consistency in human character, and the theory of the Ruling Passion alone is enough to relate the *Epistle to Cobham* to the *Essay on Man* even if nothing whatever were known of Pope's grand philosophical project of the 1730's. In fact, the discussion of the Ruling Passion in the *Essay on Man* is so much more extensive than that in the *Epistle to Cobham* that it will be instructive to consider the longer poem for a moment. In Epistle II of the *Essay* Pope has been considering the paradoxes and the psychological quirks of man as an individual, and he has already pointed out, in a memorable couplet, that

> Two principles in human nature reign:
> Self-love, to urge, and reason, to restrain.
>
> (*Essay on Man*, II, 53-54)

His development of this idea leads naturally into a further discussion of passion, which he identifies with "self-love" (II, 93), and this, in turn, leads to a comment on the bewildering variety of reactions which passion, or self-love, induces in various individuals. The pursuit of pleasure is of course one mode of self-love:

> Pleasures are ever in our hands or eyes;
> And when in act they cease, in prospect rise;
> Present to grasp, and future still to find,
> The whole employ of body and of mind.
> All spread their charms, but charm not all alike;
> On different senses different objects strike;
> Hence different passions more or less inflame,
> As strong or weak, the organs of the frame.
>
> (*Essay on Man*, II, 123-130)

This closely resembles Pope's discussion of the inconsistency and unpredictability of human nature which occupies the first 173 lines of the *Epistle to Cobham*. Then, in the very

16

next couplet of the *Essay*, the Ruling Passion is introduced as the underlying consistency which organizes and unifies the centrifugal irregularities of the lesser passions:

> And hence one master passion in the breast,
> Like Aaron's serpent, swallows up the rest.

Similarly, in the very next passage of the *Epistle to Cobham* Pope says:

> Search then the RULING PASSION: There, alone,
> The Wild are constant, and the Cunning known;
> The Fool consistent, and the False sincere;
> Priests, Princes, Women, no dissemblers here.
>
> (*Epistle to Cobham*, lines 174-177)

Having at last introduced the Ruling Passion in the *Epistle to Cobham*, Pope now explains what it can do. He points out that although human hypocrisy and inconsistency render accurate evaluations of character extremely difficult, it may nevertheless be possible to find out what individual men and women are really like by discovering the Ruling Passion which dominates the character of each. This he illustrates by means of the most interesting and detailed satiric portrait in the epistle, that of the mercurial Duke of Wharton. Wharton's Ruling Passion, Pope would have us believe, is lust for praise (line 181), a passion developed in Wharton to such fantastically irrational lengths that he cannot remain content with praise from the wise and the virtuous alone; he must needs have it from fools and knaves as well. Thus it is that the profligate duke, blessed with every gift of talent and intelligence necessary to win the esteem of worthy men, will nevertheless plunge to the uttermost depths of buffoonery and vice to gain the approbation of the contemptible. The Ruling Passion has him in its grip, and it serves to account for all the manifold aberrations of his character.

17

Concerning the Ruling Passion as Pope presents it in this epistle, Samuel Johnson wrote:

> This doctrine is in itself pernicious as well as false: its tendency is to produce the belief of a kind of moral predestination, or overruling principle which cannot be resisted; he that admits it, is prepared to comply with every desire that caprice or opportunity shall excite, and to flatter himself that he submits only to the lawful dominion of Nature, in obeying the resistless authority of his *ruling Passion*.[18]

The combination of lofty morality and plain common sense so typical of Johnson's criticism has struck close to the heart of the matter. Nevertheless, even though Johnson correctly views the Ruling Passion as a naive oversimplification, the rest of his statement is true only if he is considering the *Epistle to Cobham* as an isolated poem, apart from the *Essay on Man*. We have already seen, however, that Pope originally planned the poems as part of a larger philosophic whole, and he had already published all but the fourth epistle of the *Essay* nearly a year before the *Epistle to Cobham* was given to the public. Pope's discussion of the Ruling Passion in the *Epistle to Cobham* is therefore somewhat more meaningful if it is read in the light of what he had already said on the subject in the *Essay on Man*. The spectacle of Wharton helplessly impaled upon his Ruling Passion sounds necessitarian enough, as Johnson implies, but there is an important passage in the *Essay* (II, 161-202) which does much to dispel this necessitarian illusion—despite the earlier strictures of Crousaz. Here Pope is saying that, although the Ruling Passion cannot be denied, it can be controlled by the individual and even directed toward good and useful ends.[19] The controlling force, not unpredictably, Pope declares to be reason. The Ruling Passion

18 *The Works of Samuel Johnson, LL.D.*, 9 vols. (Oxford: Tallboys and Wheeler, 1825), VIII, 293-294.
19 Cf. *Ep. Bath.*, lines 153-160.

operates like a springboard, so to speak, which can launch a person's character in the direction of either good or ill, depending on the strength of his reason and his willingness to use it. The same Ruling Passion can produce prudence or avarice, tenderness or lust, depending on the rationality and self-control of the individual concerned. This same ambition can make one man a statesman, another a tyrant; the difference is solely that the first controls and manipulates his Ruling Passion through reason, whereas the other allows the Ruling Passion to dominate him. As Pope puts it,

> Reason the bias turns to good from ill,
> And Nero reigns a Titus, if he will.
>
> (*Essay on Man*, II, 197-198)

"If he will"—the qualification is of the utmost importance. Montaigne had said much the same thing in his essay "On the inconsistency of our actions" discussed above:

> Ambition can teach men valor, and temperance, and liberality, and even justice. Greed can implant in the heart of a shop apprentice, brought up in obscurity and idleness, the confidence to cast himself far from hearth and home, in a frail boat at the mercy of the waves and angry Neptune; it also teaches discretion and wisdom.[20]

An even more significant comment to the same effect may be found in *Spectator* No. 408, an anonymous contribution which Pope himself may possibly have written. The paper is in the form of a letter to Mr. Spectator, in which the unidentified correspondent is explaining the relationship between passion and reason in terms which curiously anticipate Pope's *Essay* of two decades later:

---

20 Montaigne, II, 8.

The strange and absurd variety that is so apparent in men's actions, shows plainly that they can never proceed from reason; so pure a fountain emits no such troubled waters. They must necessarily arise from the passions, which are to the mind as the winds to a ship, they only can move it, and they too often destroy it; if fair and gentle they guide it into the harbour, if contrary and furious they overset it in the waves. In the same manner is the mind assisted or endangered by the passions; reason must then take the place of pilot, and can never fail of securing her charge if she be not wanting to herself. The strength of the passions will never be accepted as an excuse for complying with them; they were designed for subjection, and if a man suffers them to get the upper hand, he then betrays the liberty of his own soul.

The answer to Johnson's objection lies here; to confound the Ruling Passion, as Johnson does, with libertine naturalism leads only to a serious misunderstanding of both the *Essay on Man* and the *Epistle to Cobham*. The doctrine of the Ruling Passion need not be interpreted as either necessitarian or fatalistic, and the men of the Augustan Age never intended it as a justification of untrammeled libertinism. It is perfectly possible, of course, for the Ruling Passion to unseat reason, as Pope himself admits in the *Epistle to Bathurst* (lines 155-156), but there is nothing inevitable about this. So much is entirely up to the individual. If the Duke of Wharton had only exercised reason and self-control, the lust for praise which was his Ruling Passion could have been channeled into the highest statesmanship and political achievement. As the matter stands, however, he is like the coxcomb Cleanthes in *Spectator* No. 404 (also possibly by Pope), whose great natural virtues are obscured and distorted by incessant affectation. Or, to bring Montaigne into the matter once again, "Philosophy does not think it has used its resources badly when it has given to reason the sovereign mastery of our

20

soul and the authority to hold our appetites in check" (Book II, Chapter 33, "The Story of Spurina").[21]

In the portrait of Wharton, Pope has demonstrated that the Ruling Passion, for all its crazy irrationality, is the foundation of each individual character and the sole source of predictability in human nature. This is "the naked nature" (to borrow for a moment the language of the *Essay on Criticism*, line 294), the essential unity and clarity of which are obscured, as in a bad poem, by the superficial and ancillary excrescences which immediately—but deceptively—strike the eye. It is the confusion brought about by these surface traits which renders the total personality of man "one glaring chaos and wild heap" of inconsistency. Only by shoveling all this accumulated rubbish aside can the student of human nature penetrate to the Ruling Passion beneath, and only when the Ruling Passion has been fully ascertained can a man's character be accurately evaluated.

But there still remains the danger, as we have seen, of mistaking for the true Ruling Passion a secondary trait which may arise from it but is not the same. A man may be guilty of lust or avarice (lines 210-215), for example, one or the other of which may appear superficially to be his Ruling Passion; but it may in fact be only a means of gratifying a more fundamental and deeply rooted passion. Thus the observer—especially if he does not have the stabilizing influence of general principles to support his observations—is in danger of mistaking the trees for the forest or, as Pope phrases it (line 221), "the scaffold for the pile." Again Pope is insisting, as he remarked earlier in the poem (lines 61-86), that superficial appearances are deceptive, that actions do not always reveal motives, that human character does not easily surrender itself to rational or empirical analysis. Even when the Ruling Passion may seem most clearly revealed,

---

21 Montaigne, II, 437. Cf. Pope, *Im. Hor.*, Ep. ii. 2. 278-283.

the observer may be wrong about it, for human nature, like Shylock's furtive soul (line 115), "Still sits at squat, and peeps not from its hole."

This insistence on the difficulty of ascertaining the true Ruling Passion requires those of us who would scrutinize human nature to be content with moderate hopes. Nevertheless, however inaccessible the Ruling Passion may be, it remains in constant and vigorous operation until the moment of death. Beginning at line 222 Pope concludes the epistle on this note, providing, as he goes along, a series of swiftly limned portraits by way of illustration: the "rev'rend sire" (and *sire* is a wickedly chosen word!), whose obsessive lechery persists into his dotage; the glutton Helluo, who has gorged himself to the brink of the grave and on his deathbed cries out for God's mercy and more food; "the frugal Crone," feebly trying to blow out "the hallow'd taper," miserly to the last; the vain Narcissa, whose only dying thought is of the appearance she will make in her coffin. Lustfulness, gluttony, avarice, and pride—the Ruling Passions pile up in a magnificent *stretto*, with portrait following portrait in such rapid succession that Pope seems to be reminding us still of the shifting inconsistencies of the human animal.

But despite Pope's interest in the Ruling Passion, if the *Epistle to Cobham* were nothing more than a discussion of this particular doctrine it would probably be what William Lisle Bowles (who is often unfair to Pope) and Courthope have both called it—"the worst of Pope's Epistles."[22] Even if we allow these commentators the luxury of an oversimplification, and even if we allow Johnson's point that the doctrine of the Ruling Passion is stark nonsense, the Ruling Passion is by no means all that Pope is getting at in this poem. We have already seen, in fact, that it takes him 173 lines to get to it at all. More fundamental to Pope's own nature, to

---

22 EC, 51.

the age in which he lived, and to the cause of universal truth as he saw it is his strong awareness, strikingly evident throughout the epistle, of the labyrinthine complexities of human nature. Bowles cannot be said to have grasped the clarity and incisiveness with which Pope stresses the skepticism of his attitude toward human nature and, in a larger and almost Pyrrhonian sense, toward the possibility of reaching absolute truth by any of the epistemological methods available to man. *Nosce teipsum* is easy to say but difficult to do, as much so for the race as for the individual. If we can discover a man's Ruling Passion, well and good; but at the heart of the *Epistle to Cobham* lies a dark and sobering irony, the baffling discrepancy which exists between reality and appearance and, in particular, between men as they are and men as they seem to be. The neo-classic age, and Pope with it, was forever trying to explain what it saw as the strange duality of man, equipped with reason which he all too rarely uses, hagridden with passions to which he continually succumbs—inconsistent, inscrutable, and perverse. And the dilemma becomes worse confounded when we reflect, as Pope does in various ways throughout this poem, that even those who would be thought most rational are at bottom a tissue of irrational inconsistencies. This human paradox is a common theme in the literature of neo-classicism, from the burning passions and the Jansenist conscience of Racine's Phèdre to the horrifying extremes of Yahoo and Houyhnhnm in the fourth voyage of Gulliver. Pope's most eloquent statement of this paradox is contained in the second epistle of the *Essay on Man*, in the magnificent opening lines and in those passages which attempt to find a way of reconciling passion and reason;[23] but in the *Epistle to Cobham*, a less attractive and less ambitious poem, Pope can still be seen, half ex-

23 Cf. Pascal, *Pensées*, No. 434: "Quelle chimère est-ce donc l'homme? Quelle nouveauté, quel monstre, quel chaos, quel sujet de contradiction, quel prodige! Juge de toutes choses, imbécile, ver de terre; dépositaire du vrai, cloaque d'incertitude et d'erreur; gloire et rebut de l'univers."

asperated and half amused, puzzling over the tangled con-
tradictions of his fellow men.

EPISTLE II

To a Lady

Of the Characters of Women

The *Epistle to a Lady*, the fourth and last of Pope's Moral Essays in point of publication, came out as a single poem in February 1735 (N.S.), a little more than a year after the first appearance of the *Epistle to Cobham*. When Pope gathered the four Moral Essays together for publication in the second volume of his *Works* (April 1735; Griffith 370), he placed the *Epistle to a Lady* second, presumably because its subject is closer to that of the first epistle than to that of the third and fourth (the use of riches). The version of 1735, however, is rather different from the final text of the suppressed "deathbed edition" of 1744—and therefore different also from Warburton's text of 1751—notably because the 1735 text lacks the characters of Philomedé and Cloe, the passage on Queen Caroline, and the powerful and notorious portrait of Atossa. Since Pope's original manuscript of the poem is lost (Bateson notes that two autograph manuscripts were sold at Christie's as late as 1889),[24] it is nearly impossible to say how much of this material was in it and how much was composed later on. The description of Cloe (lines 157-180) first appeared under the title "Cloe: a Character" in the 1738 edition of Pope's *Works* (published May 1739) (Vol. II, Part ii; Griffith 507). The date of composition of the other three cannot be determined either, but their highly scandalous nature probably precluded their publication while the individuals concerned were still alive. By 1744, however, all these women were dead—if we assume that the Duchess of Marlborough was *not* the original of Atossa—and Pope could therefore feel some justification in publishing the portraits. Bateson believes, with some reason,

---

24 TE, 39, fn. 2.

that the portraits were all part of the original manuscripts and that delicacy, or prudence, dictated their suppression during the 1730's.[25] Brief comments on the identity of each of these ladies will be found in the notes.

The *Epistle to a Lady* may conveniently be grouped with the *Epistle to Cobham,* for the obvious and rather superficial reason that its subject, in the final analysis, is the inconsistency of human nature. The present poem, however, is much more specifically concerned with the female character as distinguished from the male than *To Cobham* is with men as distinguished from women. The foregoing discussion of the *Epistle to Cobham* has touched upon this point, and the comparison suggested there between the Arguments of the two poems provides a further clarification of the distinction. The Argument of the first epistle refers always to man as a human being, rather than as a male, and women are never mentioned in the Argument at all. The Argument of the *Epistle to a Lady,* however, announces the subject of the poem to be ". . . the Characters of *Women* (considered only as contra-distinguished from the other Sex)." (The italics are Pope's.) It is hardly surprising to find Pope saying next "That these [i.e., the characters of women] are yet more inconsistent and incomprehensible than those of Men. . . ." Human nature, as we have already seen in the *Epistle to Cobham,* is inconsistent enough and difficult enough to fathom at the best of times, but when the person under observation is a woman—more especially when she is a depraved and hypocritical woman—the inconsistency becomes so perniciously irrational as to warrant exposure in a poem:

> Whether the Charmer sinner it, or saint it,
> If Folly grow romantic, I must paint it.

> (*Epistle to a Lady,* lines 15-16)

---

25 TE, 41-42.

This couplet is not quite so lighthearted as it may appear, for Pope is using the word *romantic* as the neo-classic period generally understood it, in its older sense of "fantastic, extravagant, quixotic; going beyond what is rational or practical"(*OED*). The folly on which Pope is concentrating in this epistle, then, is folly become grotesque and often wicked —the filth of Sappho, the pseudo-intellectual promiscuities of Philomedé, the towering rages of the terrible Atossa. Even the names which Pope assigns to some of the principal characters serve to bear out this impression of fantastic irrationality. Apart from the standard pastoral sobriquets conventional in this kind of poetry (Narcissa, Cloe, etc.) Pope has provided at least two which are far from standard: Philomedé, apparently a coinage, which means literally "a lover of the Medes" and hence a lover of all things barbarous and eccentric; and Atossa, the name of the woman who was the sister and also the wife of the mad and drunken Cambyses of Persia (d. ca. 522 B.C.). The characters in the *Epistle to a Lady* thus bear strong traces of madness and evil, and for this reason the obvious temptation to identify the poem with Pope's other satire of "the sex," *The Rape of the Lock*, should be resisted. Only in those passages which are not specifically satirical (lines 1-20, 249-292) does the *Epistle to a Lady* approach the geniality and the rococo lightness of the earlier poem. With the possible exception of Papillia (lines 37-40) and the splendid lines on the aged beauties (lines 219-248), the satirical portraits of this epistle are noticeably more scathing than gallant. Belinda, in *The Rape of the Lock*, has her own foibles and inconsistencies (the very genesis of that poem is rooted in folly); but Belinda, after all, is a young girl whose charm is hard to resist even when she is most exasperating. Admittedly she is silly, but she is young enough to be fresh, harmless, and relatively innocent. In Philomedé and Narcissa, however, the pretty foibles of Belinda have been coarsened and frozen into gargoyles. What is inconsistency in her has

become perversity in them; the pleasant flirtations of fifteen
have been transformed into the callous debaucheries of thirty-
five. It is one of the perennial tragedies of human life that
the Belindas of today are all too often the Philomedés and
Atossas of tomorrow, and the difference between them ac-
counts for the difference in tone between the two poems.

The inconsistency of the feminine character, then, is the
subject of the *Epistle to a Lady*, an inconsistency which is
always baffling and sometimes horrible. The tensions which
it produces are exploited by Pope with all the subtle skill in
portraiture at his command; indeed, the paradoxical satiric
portraits which follow one another in swift succession throughout the epistle betray Pope's lifelong interest in painting. At
the very beginning of the poem he launches his discussion
of feminine inconsistency by commenting on a fad popular
among the fashionable ladies of his generation, their fondness
for having their portraits painted in all manner of poses,
characters, and attitudes, from the pomp of a duchess to the
arch simplicity of a milkmaid:

> How many pictures of one Nymph we view,
> All how unlike each other, all how true!
> Arcadia's Countess, here, in ermin'd pride,
> Is there, Pastora by a fountain side.
> Here Fannia, leering on her own good man,
> And there, a naked Leda with a Swan

> (Lines 5-10)

The Countess of Pembroke ("Arcadia's Countess"), portrayed
now in the formal regalia of her rank, now in the simple
garb of a shepherdess, is a harmless enough example of this
inconsistency; but in the very next couplet Pope clearly implies corruption. Fannia (whoever she may have been) is
likewise shown by the painter in two different poses, but
one of them is at least implicitly lascivious, the other patently

28

so. In the first, the chill participle *leering* dashes at once the little picture of domestic bliss which the painter has ostensibly portrayed; and in the second pose, with its voluptuous baroque exhibitionism reminiscent of Tintoretto, Fannia's depravity is made quite overt. The same hypocritical duality of superficial virtue and secret sin is brilliantly captured in the next four lines, which describe two other feminine portraits:

> Let then the Fair one beautifully cry,
> In Magdalen's loose hair and lifted eye,
> Or drest in smiles of sweet Cecilia shine,
> With simp'ring Angels, Palms, and Harps divine.

(Lines 11-14)

This neat shift from the pseudo-classical to the pseudo-Christian does not change the underlying hypocrisy in the least. The mere desire of a lady of fashion to be painted as Saint Mary Magdalen implies no such genuine piety as was hers; the emphasis is clearly on the brazen ogling of the prostitute rather than the tears of the soulstruck penitent. The double meaning of the adjective *loose* and the pointedly ambiguous "lifted eye" are of obvious significance in this regard. Similarly, although a lady may fancy herself alluring in the guise of Saint Cecilia, the smiles that finally emerge upon the canvas are those of a wanton, and the angels in the background are simpering like any bawd. *Simp'ring*, a perfect word, does for Pope's innuendo here exactly what *leering* does for the line describing the portrait of Fannia and her own good man. The whole passage may at first glance seem nothing more than another example of the graceful rococo elegance which Pope's detractors like to describe as his only achievement, but it is far more subtle and suggestive than this. The paintings themselves are worthy of Watteau at his most devastating, especially through the insight they provide into a fashionable society which is idle, useless, and spiritually barren. The

29

deftness of Pope's psychological penetration enables these lines to perform to the very letter their function of introducing a major theme of Pope's satire in this epistle, hypocrisy as a significant form of human—and in this instance female—inconsistency. Thus, what we have seen as perhaps the major idea underlying the *Epistle of Cobham,* the discrepancy between people as they appear and as they really are, is introduced at the outset in the present poem. The fact that the idea is presented philosophically in the first epistle and dramatically and satirically in this one provides a positive clue to the relative unpopularity of the *Epistle to Cobham*

This feminine hypocrisy is reinforced in the very next passage, itself a masterpiece of rococo humor and grace—but with a point. The point is that Pope is here equating hypocrisy and pretense with artificiality as well as inconsistency; and, since he has been speaking all along in terms of painting, he expands the metaphor even further and adds the slightest touch of another kind of painting as well:

> Come then, the colours and the ground prepare!
> Dip in the Rainbow, trick her off in Air;
> Chuse a firm Cloud, before it fall, and in it
> Catch, e'er she change, the Cynthia of this minute.

> (Lines 17-20)

The veiled allusion to cosmetics in the first line of this passage is quite in the rococo vein of *The Rape of the Lock,* and it strongly implies not only artificiality but change. This subtle hint of inconsistency is then strengthened by the double meaning attached to the verb *fall,* the sly insistence that the cloud be a firm one, and the suggestion that although a woman may be chaste ("Cynthia") this minute, what the next few seconds may bring could be quite another matter. And the probable shortness of this interval of chastity is neatly caught by the light monosyllables and the quick, mincing feminine endings of the second couplet, where *in it* rhymes with *minute* like the tick of a lady's watch.

In the first twenty lines of the epistle, then, Pope has established his theme by showing in a remarkable variety of ways that woman is a changeable, inconstant, Protean creature; and despite the charm and grace of the poetry, his implication of an underlying depravity has prepared the reader fully for most of the terrible revelations which are to come. They follow at once, in a more or less ascending scale of inconsistency—the richly bejeweled Sappho, who never takes a bath; the soft, frail Silia, suddenly erupting in a pimple and a tantrum; the fickle Papillia; the oddly bewitching Calypso—until finally the first of the three great grotesques is ushered in with the bone-chilling couplet

> Narcissa's nature, tolerably mild,
> To make a wash, would hardly stew a child.
>
> (Lines 53-54)

Narcissa's magnanimous forbearance in the preparation of her skin lotion introduces a woman whose good nature is largely caprice and whose caprices, in turn, run to the most fantastic extremes of stark asceticism and abandoned vice. These two extremes, conscience and passion, between which Narcissa continually fluctuates strike a characteristically neo-classic note and introduce by implication the Golden Mean, which we have already seen by suggestion in the *Epistle to Cobham* and which is to receive more explicit treatment in the *Epistle to Bathurst*. There is thus a very real sense in which Narcissa, torn in a raging conflict between flesh and spirit, is a clear embodiment of the human dilemma as the neo-classic age saw it; she is thus a condensed version of the tragic heroine of Racine's *Phèdre*. This parallel is especially close in the pathos of the concluding couplet of the portrait, where Narcissa is described as

> A very Heathen in the carnal part,
> Yet still a sad, good Christian at her heart.

(Lines 67-68)

The implication is that Narcissa, like Phèdre, cannot help herself. The love of pleasure, one of the two great Ruling Passions which Pope later ascribes to women (lines 207-210), holds her firmly in its grasp, and her reason is powerless to combat it.

Less venial, because it is more hypocritically ugly, is the depravity of Philomedé, who now staggers into the poem in a mock-heroic and magnificently scornful couplet:

> See Sin in State, majestically drunk;
> Proud as a Peeress, prouder as a Punk.

(Lines 69-70)

The reeling solemnity—obvious in the rhythms—of this statuesque and inebriate Juno is laughably incongruous, but this is not the worst of it. Darkened as it is by the blandly sanctimonious air which she affects in public, her inconsistency is more sophisticated and more dishonest than the relatively simple extremes of poor Narcissa. Philomedé preaches in the drawing room the virtues of "the soft passion and the Taste refin'd"; yet she makes the seclusion of her own boudoir the scene of the coarsest of pleasures indulged with the most vulgar of partners. Thus she is living proof of Pope's later statement that ". . . ev'ry Woman is at heart a Rake" (line 216), but her tastes are degraded and her refinements merely assumed. She is an aged and morally thickened version of Belinda.

There follow numerous other examples of feminine inconsistency in various forms (the "wits and refiners" and the "stupid and silly," as Pope calls them, Dante-fashion, in his Argument), but these are summarily dismissed. They scatter like sparrows before the fearful advent of "great Atossa," a really frightening creation, who, in the fury of her anger, "Finds all her life one warfare upon earth," who

> From loveless youth to unrespected age,
> No Passion gratify'd except her Rage.
>
> (Lines 125-126)

The word *creation* must be stressed in any discussion of this woman, for too much has been made of the mere identity of Atossa among Pope's acquaintance and correspondingly little of the strength of the passage as piece of creative, imaginative portraiture—as though Pope in his satiric portraits did nothing but take photographs. It would, of course, be interesting to ascertain whether the lines were intended for Sarah, Duchess of Marlborough, or the equally formidable Catharine, Duchess of Buckinghamshire—the description, in general outline, seems to fit them both equally well—but this is not the main point. What Pope has really achieved in this character is something that T. S. Eliot once charged him with being unable to do:[26] he has created a portrait which, far from being a mere miniature, is magnified to the point where it is larger and more terrible than life itself. Throughout the passage Pope strikes home with ruthless effect by isolating the characteristic in question and turning upon it the glaring light of exaggeration, much as Swift isolated pettiness and nobility, reason and unreason, in *Gulliver's Travels.* Pope's very language is furious here: *Knaves, Fools, hates, whisks, Fool* again, *Passion, Rage, Fury, Revenge from*

---

26 In his essay "John Dryden" (1921).

Hell, storm, Hate again, *Passion* again, *hate* a third time, *death, curse, hate* once more, *curs'd* again—all within the space of thirty-five lines. And Atossa's behavior, as Pope presents it, lurches constantly between extremes—extremes which not only surpass the merely unreasonable but verge on lunacy. Atossa is consistent only in the gargantuan violence of her passions, passions which flare up with little or no provocation and for virtually no reason that a rational mind can fathom. The total picture is of a creature so dreadful, so appallingly grotesque, described in language so harsh and brutal, that it reads in nearly every detail like a page out of Dante's *Inferno*.[27] In the face of this masterpiece of controlled fury it is fruitless to wonder whom the lines were intended to portray (the point is mentioned in the notes), although the fact that they were intended to portray someone is evident from their suppression until 1744. The important consideration for critical purposes is that Pope has achieved in the character of Atossa a brilliant and lurid portrait and a remarkable feat of epic hyperbole. To borrow the phrase which Eliot used in commendation of Dryden, these lines "create the object that they contemplate."[28] What they create is a picture of human nature riven and distorted by unbridled passion into a condition not far removed from emotional Yahooism.

From this fearful climax Pope slides gradually downhill until, by means of a skillful transition (lines 193-200), he has placed himself in a position to compare men and women on some important general points. One of these is the Ruling Passion (lines 207-218, the only place in the poem where it is mentioned), which usually appears in women, Pope says, in only two forms—"The Love of Pleasure, and the Love

---

27 Cf. *Im. Donne*, IV, 192-193:
     Not Dante, dreaming all th'infernal state,
     Beheld such scenes of envy, sin, and hate.
28 *Loc. cit.*

of Sway" (line 210). This leads smoothly into the wonderful
tragi-comedy of the superannuated belles, in whom the youthful modesty which formerly served to cloak their indiscre-
tions has given way in age to a pathetic pretense of non-
existent intrigues. Herein lies their inconsistency:

> At last, to follies Youth could scarce defend,
> It grows their Age's prudence to pretend;
> Asham'd to own they gave delight before,
> Reduc'd to feign it, when they give no more.

> (Lines 235-238)

The Ruling Passion here, Pope would have us believe, is the
love of pleasure. The depth to which this is ingrained in
such women is hinted by the sly and paradoxical insertion
of the noun *prudence* in line 236. Such a pretense is of
course not prudent at all, but the Ruling Passion (the love of
pleasure) is so strong that its influence remains pervasive
long after all hope of gratifying it is gone. Like the veteran
politicians in the *Epistle to Cobham* (lines 248-251), these
veteran charmers cannot face the harsh reality that they have
outlasted their only *raison d'être* and that their lives are consequently devoid of essential meaning. But the Ruling Passion
persists blindly and doggedly until the last, as Pope has told
us in the first epistle, and

> As Hags hold Sabbaths, less for joy than spight,
> So these their merry, miserable Night;
> Still round and round the Ghosts of Beauty glide,
> And haunt the places where their Honour dy'd.

> (Lines 239-242)

Here again is Belinda grown old. The description is psychologi-
cally sound (whether or not the theory of the Ruling Passion
is), and the misery of these feckless and tormented souls is

intensified by a veiled reminiscence of Plato's *Phaedo* which may not be entirely accidental. But at once, lest the temptation to sympathize with these faded beauties grow too strong, Pope shatters the hushed sorrow of his rococo vision with an abrupt reminder that the lives of such women are totally empty and useless. The passage is one of the finest examples in Pope of the Augustan balance, symmetry, and compression:

> See how the World its Veterans rewards!
> A Youth of Frolicks, an old Age of Cards;
> Fair to no purpose, artful to no end,
> Young without Lovers, old without a Friend;
> A Fop their Passion, but their Prize a Sot,
> Alive, ridiculous, and dead, forgot!

(Lines 243-248)

With these devastating lines Pope has reached the end of his portrait gallery of feminine inconsistency. The inconsistencies have embraced both the individual and the type and have run the gamut from relatively harmless frivolity and fickleness (Papillia) to the hypocrisy of Philomedé and the unpredictable violence of Atossa. At intervals throughout the poem (notably lines 151-156 and 181-198) Pope has reminded his reader of the basic controlling metaphor with which he began, that of the poet as painter, of the satiric character sketch as a study in oils on canvas. Now, at line 249, he turns directly once again to Martha Blount, the lady to whom he is writing, and addresses her as the model of all that is most sensible and lovable in feminine inconsistency. For inconsistency, consistently enough, is not confined to the vicious, the hypocritical, and the silly among women; it dominates the sex and can operate for better as well as for worse. Fundamental to this assertion is Pope's statement (lines 269-280) that Heaven's "last best work," the ideal human creature, is a judicious blend of feminine and masculine qualities, uniting "Your Taste of Follies, with our Scorn of Fools," "Courage with Softness, Modesty with Pride"—an androgynous mixture of Belinda and Bolingbroke which closely approximates the Golden Mean. And this rare creature, Pope gallantly implies, is Martha Blount herself: Heaven selects the strength of men and the elusive fascinations of women, "Shakes all together, and produces—You" (line 280). What this ideal combination amounts to is the double virtue of sense and good humor on the possession of which Pope congratulates his lady in the concluding line of the poem. Just as reason and common sense can direct the Ruling Passion toward benign and useful ends (as Pope makes clear in the *Epistle to Bathurst*, lines 153-160, and in the second epistle of the *Essay on Man*), so the vagaries of women can be redeemed by these same saving graces until the very inconsistency which Atossa's "enthusiasm" has turned into a nightmare becomes in a reasonable woman the source of all her charm.

With "Patty" Blount (as her friends called her) Pope was on terms of considerable intimacy, and his address to her is a perfect example of the warmth and generosity which formed a very real part of his own nature. This capacity for friendship in Pope, which he never hesitated to display in verse toward those whom he liked and trusted, has all too often been overshadowed by the more sensational traits of malevolence and nastiness with which his detractors have never wearied of charging him. To accuse of "malignancy and insincerity" (the words are Macaulay's)[29] the author of the conclusion to the *Epistle to a Lady*, or for that matter of the great tributes to Bolingbroke, Arbuthnot, Gay, and Swift in Pope's poetry, is to take a onesided and self-righteous view of a highly complex character, one whom it is better to try to understand than merely to attack.

---

29 In his essay "The Life and Writings of Addison."

EPISTLE III

To Allen Lord Bathurst

The *Epistle to Bathurst* was the second of Pope's Moral Essays in point of publication and, with its 402 lines, is by far the longest of the four. Like the other three epistles, it appeared originally as a separate book and was published for the first time on January 15, 1733 (N. S.), in folio form (Griffith 280). The poem is also the most difficult and thematically complex of the Moral Essays, and Pope admitted to Swift, in a letter dated exactly a month after the appearance of the folio (February 16, 1733) that the *Epistle to Bathurst* had cost him more pains than any other poem he had yet written.[30] There were other problems as well. The reception accorded the *Epistle to Burlington*, published little more than a year earlier, had been a source of great vexation and embarrassment to Pope, owing to the malicious and unwarranted identification of the character of Timon in that poem with the Duke of Chandos (see *Epistle to Burlington*, line 99 and note 38). In a poem published only a few weeks after *To Bathurst*, Pope made angry reference to the subject:

> [F.] Ev'n those you touch not, hate you.
>   *P.* What should ail 'em?
>   *F.* A hundred smart in *Timon* and in *Balaam*:
> The fewer still you name, you wound the more;
> *Bond* is but one, but *Harpax* is a score.

> (*Im. Hor.*, Sat. ii. 1. 41-44)

Pope, in all likelihood, had also protested the invidious misconstruction of *To Burlington* in an unpublished and unsigned prose satire, "A Master Key to Popery," written probably no

---

30 *Corr*, III, 348.

later than February 1732 (N. S.) and discovered in the late 1940's by Professor John Butt among the papers of the Duke of Devonshire.[31] It is therefore not surprising that the present epistle should betray further evidence of Pope's disgust, for in many instances he used real names (though at first with some letters omitted) instead of pseudo-classical sobriquets for many of the individuals whom he meant to satirize. Although it was not to be very long before he would revert to pseudonyms once again, Pope expressed his annoyance in a letter to Burlington dated January 1732 (N. S.), only a few weeks after the publication of *To Burlington*:

> I have learnt that there are some who would rather be wicked than ridiculous; and therefore it may be safer to attack vices than follies. I will therefore leave my betters in the quiet possession of their idols, their groves, and their high places; and change my subject from their pride to their meanness, from their vanities to their miseries; and as the only certain way to avoid misconstructions, to lessen offence, and not to multiply ill-natured applications, I may probably, in my next [i. e., *To Bathurst*], make use of real names instead of fictitious ones.[32]

This letter has the further interest of suggesting the nature of the relationship between the two epistles on the use of riches and, at the same time, of providing another clue to Pope's reasons for adopting the order in which the four Moral Essays have always appeared since the editions of 1735. (See the introduction to the *Epistle to Cobham*, pp. 9-10 above.) As the epistles to Cobham and Martha Blount form in some sense a pair on the general subject of human inconsistency, so those to Bathurst and Burlington

---

31 John Butt, "A Master Key to Popery," *Pope and His Contemporaries: Essays Presented to George Sherburn*, ed. James L. Clifford and Louis A. Landa (Oxford: The Clarendon Press, 1949), pp. 45-57.

32 Warburton, 215. The letter is reprinted in *Corr*, III, 265-266.

form a pair on the proper use of wealth. The two latter are related in that they deal with two opposite and irrational extremes in the handling of money: *To Burlington* (written first) is a satire on extravagance; *To Bathurst* is an attack on avarice in all its forms—the avarice of the miser, the usurer, the gambler, the speculator—although there are distinct overtones of prodigality in the poem as well. Thus the two epistles, taken together, represent another of Pope's many examinations of the human tendency to go to extremes and another of his many comments on the desirability of the Golden Mean. At the same time, the two poems assert in the strongest terms Pope's belief that the rich have an obligation to assist those less fortunate than they (cf. *Epistle to Bathurst*, lines 219-236). From him to whom much is given, much will be expected, but this fact both miser and spendthrift alike have refused to acknowledge.

Earl R. Wasserman's elaborate study of the *Epistle to Bathurst* has documented from Renaissance, patristic, and Scriptural sources the elements of Christian doctrine which lend to this poem something of the character of a Christian sermon.[33] With the patently classical features of the poem —Horatian familiarity and mock-epic satire, Stoic asceticism and the Golden Mean—Pope has combined an attack on avarice and usury which, as we shall see, has something in common with the traditions of medieval Catholic Christianity. Viewed in this light, the *Epistle to Bathurst*, as Professor Wasserman points out, is both Christian sermon and Horatian *sermo*. Although no one doubts the strong classical bent of much of Pope's poetry, such Christian elements as appear in the present poem are quite as important, especially in view of the strong emphasis which such commentators as Crousaz have placed on his supposedly heterodox opinions.

---

33 Earl R. Wasserman, *Pope's Epistle to Bathurst: A Critical Reading with an Edition of the Manuscripts* (Baltimore: The Johns Hopkins Press, 1960), pp. 12-13 (hereinafter cited as Wasserman).

Samuel Johnson, who was by no means fully persuaded of Pope's orthodoxy, remarks that Pope's Roman Catholicism is more strongly hinted in the *Epistle to Bathurst* than in any other poem.[34] This is borne out, as Johnson observes, by the derisive description of young Cotta at the head of the London "enthusiasts" as they burn the Pope in effigy (lines 213-214) and by Pope's obvious indignation at the anti-Catholic libels inscribed on the base of the Monument (lines 339-340 and note). Johnson might also have mentioned the brief slur cast at the anti-Catholic Coningsby (line 397) and, most important of all for purposes of the present discussion, the implied anti-Puritanism of Pope's attack on parsimony and greed.

At the same time, however, Pope cannot be regarded as a poet in whom specific theology looms large. The scant references to his own religion in Pope's poetry[35] do not tell us a great deal about his theological convictions, if indeed he had any, and he is by no means so strongly anti-Puritan as Dryden. In general, he seems to have thought of himself as a Roman Catholic of the Erasmus type—liberal, moderate, and undogmatic:

> Papist or Protestant, or both between,
> Like good Erasmus in an honest Mean.

> (*Im. Hor.*, Sat. ii. 1. 65-66)

This may be the statement of an honest man, but it is not necessarily that of a zealous or devout one. It is the statement of a poet who, as Pope's work shows, is less interested in promoting specific theological viewpoints than in advancing the cause of rational and ethical behavior among his fellow men. Even his theodicy in the *Essay on Man*, orthodox though

---

34 Johnson, VIII, 292.
35 Cf. *Im. Donne*, II, 105-108; IV, 34-35, 256-257; *Dunciad*, III, 283-284.

some of it is, has strong overtones of the universal system of ethics which, to the deists, formed the substance of all religion. The primarily ethical tendencies of what passed for religion with Pope are indicated in a letter which he wrote to his friend Francis Atterbury, Bishop of Rochester, on November 20, 1717:

> After all, I verily believe your lordship and I are both of the same religion, if we were thoroughly understood by one another, and that all honest and reasonable Christians would be so, if they did but talk together every day; and had nothing to do together, but to serve God, and live in peace with their neighbors.[36]

The *Epistle to Bathurst,* despite the thinly veiled allusions to Roman Catholic belief which it contains, is concerned with ethical problems, specifically with avarice and parsimony; but these are sins which many non-Christian thinkers have unequivocally denounced. Aristotle, in Book IV of the *Ethics* (1122a), equates usurers with gamblers and brothel-keepers in that their common characteristic is the love of base gain. A passage in the Koran (II, 276) comes very close to the heart of Pope's poem: "Allah hath blighted usury and made almsgiving fruitful."[37] Usury is explicitly forbidden, and charity is demanded, by the law of Moses (Lev. 25:35-37), and God's wrath upon the people of Jerusalem for violating this law is declared in explicit terms by the prophet Ezekiel (22:12). There is nothing exclusively Christian, then, in the attack on avarice and misuse of money; in Pope's own attack he is trying once again to come to terms with the kind of problem that really interested him, a universal problem in ethics and human behavior. Of course, Pope is speak-

---

36 EC, V, 246; *Corr,* I, 454.
37 *The Meaning of the Glorious Koran,* trans. Mohammed Marmaduke Pickthall (New York: New American Library, 1953), p. 59. Cf. also III, 130; IV, 161; XXX, 39.

ing in this poem as a Christian, not as a Greek or a Jew or a Mohammedan, and he is writing for readers who knew their Bible; but those same readers also knew their Aristotle and their Horace and their Vergil.

The *Epistle to Bathurst* contains a number of Biblical allusions, most of them from the Old Testament; and in Pope's sustained attack on the stock-jobbing, money-grubbing propensities of his age there is more than a hint of Old Testament wrath. He is strongly suspicious of the profit motive, especially when it takes the form of speculation, usury, and graft, as it did so scandalously in the South Sea bubble and the equally notorious Charitable Corporation for the Relief of the Industrious Poor. Pope's annoyance at the cupidity of his fellow countrymen is expressed in a famous passage from a poem published five years later:

> Here, Wisdom calls: "Seek Virtue first! be bold!
> "As Gold to Silver, Virtue is to Gold."
> There, London's voice: "Get Mony, Mony still!
> "And then let Virtue follow, if she will."
> This, this the saving doctrine, preach'd to all,
> From low St. James's up to high St. Paul.

> (*Im. Hor.*, Ep. i. 1. 77-82)

If Pope does not go so far as to argue, with Dante, that usury is a crime against "art," that is, against the justly profitable labor of the artisan, he does agree with the medieval view of money as sterile and unproductive in itself. Only when money is used for worthy purposes does it take on genuine value (cf. *Epistle to Burlington*, line 179), and Pope insists that the ability to amass and store away great quantities of wealth is no necessary token of God's Grace. Pope is attacking the Puritan belief advanced by Calvin that wealth *per se* is a mark of Christian virtue, together with its almost inevitable corollary, that poverty must somehow be a penance

44

inflicted by Divine Judgment upon the idle and improvident. Avarice and financial chicanery were commonly regarded, at least by those who disliked the Whigs and the Protestant sectaries, as typically Puritan vices, and Pope takes such an anti-Puritan stand near the beginning of his poem. He has adopted, for purposes of argument, the philosophical attitude of a Christian moralist writing to a confirmed cynic; but he declares that, however their beliefs may differ on other subjects, he and Bathurst are in substantial agreement on at least one point:

> Both fairly owning, Riches, in effect,
> No grace of Heav'n or token of th' Elect.
>
> (*Epistle to Bathurst*, lines 17-18)

The phrasing of the second line, in particular, indicates well enough the anti-Puritan spirit in which Pope, a Tory and a nominal Roman Catholic, is addressing Bathurst, a Tory and a philosophical cynic. It is significant that Bathurst can share Pope's anti-Puritan views on the moral implications of wealth and that he shares them, we are forced to conclude, on purely ethical, rather than specifically theological, grounds.

Pope's identification of the economic virtues with the Puritan ethic is similar to that which R. H. Tawney was to make two centuries later. Tawney points out in *Religion and the Rise of Capitalism* (1926) that the Calvinist movement had its origin in an urban and mercantile environment and that Calvin did not recognize the medieval distrust of profit or the medieval assumption that God might sometimes look with favor upon the deserving poor. Tawney writes:

> [Calvinism] no longer suspects the whole world of economic motive as alien to the life of the spirit, or distrusts the capitalist as one who has necessarily grown rich on the misfortunes of his neighbor, or

45

regards poverty in itself as meritorious, and it is perhaps the first systematic body of religious teaching which can be said to recognize and applaud the economic virtues. Its enemy is not the accumulation of riches, but their misuse for purposes of self-indulgence or ostentation.[38]

This passage significantly illuminates Pope's thesis in the present poem, and the last sentence, as the *Epistle to Burlington* shows, is one with which Pope himself would have heartily concurred. In the *Epistle to Bathurst*, however, Pope's attitude is that those who "recognize and applaud the economic virtues" have a pernicious tendency to carry their recognition and applause too far. It therefore comes to pass that a man like Denis Bond, of the Charitable Corporation, "damns the Poor, and hates them from his heart" (line 102); that Sir Gilbert Heathcote, Governor of the Bank of England, "holds it for a rule" that "ev'ry man in want is knave or fool" (lines 103-104); that Sir John Blunt, of the South Sea Corporation, can heartlessly declare, "God cannot love the wretch he starves" (lines 105-106). As Tawney puts it,

Convinced that character is all and circumstances nothing, [the Puritan] sees in the poverty of those who fall by the way, not a misfortune to be pitied and relieved, but a moral failing to be condemned, and in riches, not an object of suspicion—though like other gifts they may be abused—but the blessing which rewards the triumph of energy and will.[39]

The lack of compassion described by Pope and Tawney stands in ironic contrast to the teachings of Christ and the Apostles or, in the Moral Essays, to the loving charity of the Man of Ross (lines 249-283) and to the munificence of Lord Burl-

---

38 R. H. Tawney, *Religion and the Rise of Capitalism* (New York: New American Library, 1947), pp. 93-94.

39 Tawney, p. 191.

ington in the fourth of these epistles. Pope and Bathurst have agreed, therefore, that money is in fact morally neutral and has no character either good or bad in itself. This is precisely the attitude of medieval Christianity; it is no accident that Dante placed the usurers in his *Inferno* next to the sodomites on a desert of burning sand, for both, in their way, have sinned by devoting their productive energies to unnaturally barren pursuits.

Pope, then, refuses to accept the bland assumption of some Puritans that riches are an automatic guarantee of moral or ethical superiority. Wealth may be acquired by good men and evil men alike, as the Stoics insisted, and that which comes indifferently to both the good and the evil cannot be regarded as a good. In fact, characteristic of the balance which Pope seems instinctively to maintain in this poem between Christian and pre-Christian ethics is the Stoic belief expressed in the very next couplet. Riches are

> Giv'n to the Fool, the Mad, the Vain, the Evil,
> To Ward, to Waters, Chartres, and the Devil.
>
> (Lines 19-20)

This is a distinct echo of Seneca's essay "On Providence":

> Riches are not a good; that is why the pimp Elius must have riches, so that men who sanctify money in temples may see that it is in the brothel also. God can discredit the objects of our concupiscence in no more effective way than by bestowing them upon vile characters and withholding them from the best.[40]

And in the very Stoic fourth epistle of the *Essay on Man* (published a year after *To Bathurst*), Pope was to say the very same thing again:

---

40 *The Stoic Philosophy of Seneca*, trans. Moses Hadas (Garden City, N. Y.: Doubleday and Co., Inc., 1958), p. 40. Cf. Ps. 73:12.

The good or bad the gifts of Fortune gain,
But these less taste them, as they worse obtain.

(*Essay on Man*, IV, 83-84)

There follows a statement (which Warburton turned into a dialogue) concerning the uses and abuses of money (lines 29-34): "Useful, I grant, it serves what life requires" (Pope says), but when money is abused it can and does engender the horrors of treachery, graft, and even murder. This forms a skillful transition into one of the most brilliant pieces of whimsy in an otherwise somber indictment of human greed—though Pope, as a moralist, never loses sight of the object of his attack even when, as a poet, he is most enjoying himself. In these lines Pope speculates fancifully on the inconveniences which would obstruct every effort at bribery and corruption if there were no such thing as money and if bribes and gambling debts, consequently, had to be paid in kind. The passage soon rises to the ludicrous incongruity of mock-epic, as Pope imagines the notorious gamesters of the day (here the Duke of Bedford and the Earl of Bristol) parading to White's Club to gamble, not with money but with such encumbrances as bulls, horses, and other prizes ordinarily associated with epic games (lines 55-60). Pope is here setting up an ironic contrast between the glorious athletic contests of classical epic and the sordid, sterile gaming of White's Club, where the contest is drunken and sedentary and the prize mere *turpe lucrum*. The resulting incongruity is not only funny in itself; it is a biting commentary on both the sterility of money and the moral and physical flabbiness of Pope's age.

The very awkwardness of the bribes and the gambling stakes in this passage (lines 35-64) is packed with suggestion. The clumsiness of the bull, kicking and butting in the crowded gaming rooms at White's, intensifies the grotesqueries of the picture; and the mock-pathos of Uxorio's lady, weeping in helpless rage at the six whores (not one, but six) whom her husband has won at cards, is satire which succeeds in being personal and universal, fantastic and deadly serious, all at the same time. And the obvious superfluity of six whores is simultaneously a sardonic comment on the accumulation of surplus wealth and a reflection of the gambler's immoral abuse of money, as he strives to make artificially fertile that which is naturally sterile. (We have already observed that Aristotle groups prostitution, gambling, and usury together in a single category of base gain.) These points are further reinforced by the introduction of Lord Hervey's swine—a whole herd of them—which not only form a vivid contrast to his own perfumed delicacy but symbolize once again the ugly abuse of money squandered in enormous quantities for purposes of mere sport (lines 61-62). Viewed in the light of these symbols, the whole passage provides a brilliant summary of the objects of Pope's attack in this epistle: the dirtiness of the sin of avarice, which hoards surplus funds and renders them useless for either charity or hospitality, and the equally ugly abuse of money to make more money, an abuse in which gambling is clearly akin to usury and speculation. By inflating the object of man's cupidity from something easily carried in purse or pocket to something which has to be driven bellowing along the streets, Pope's mock-epic treatment has both magnified and rendered concrete the sin of avarice itself and has thus exposed it forcefully and wittily to the glare of public scrutiny.

As matters actually stand, however, money exists. The development of money as an easy medium of exchange has turned bribery, gambling, and all kinds of financial corruption into relatively simple and clandestine transactions. And, what is even worse, man's endless ingenuity in facilitating his own wickedness has made graft even more convenient through the highly efficient device of credit, which Pope now ironically apostrophizes:

> Blest paper-credit! last and best supply!
> That lends Corruption lighter wings to fly!

(Lines 69-70)

Pope's poetry, intentionally heavy in the gambling passage, now begins to soar as he describes with ironic glee the ease and secrecy with which the most enormous corruptions can be carried out by means of a single sheet of paper (lines 75-78). Like the bulls and coursers and whores of the mock-epic games at White's, the bill of credit is swollen to heroic significance until it becomes one of the Sibylline leaves described by Vergil in the prophecy of Helenus at Buthrotum (*Aeneid* iii. 445-452). Again the allusion is full of indirect suggestion. As the Sibyl of Cumae carelessly allows her priceless prophecies to blow away on the wind, and *inconsulti abeunt sedemque odere Sibyllae*, so heads of state in Pope's own age scatter just as recklessly the "fates and fortunes" of their subjects for the sake of personal aggrandizement and thus incur the hatred of whole nations. And the reference to the Sibyl is further filled out with an appropriate suggestion of the magical, for this tiny scrap of paper, flitting through the air on the slightest breeze, is heavy with importance: like the Sibylline prophecy which it resembles, it carries with it the fate of multitudes.

After this remarkable flight of mock-epic fancy, Pope returns to sober reality and begins to inquire into the basic and legitimate purposes which money can serve. These he finds, in the austere mood of *Piers Plowman*, to be nothing more than the necessities of life—food, clothing, and warmth, with a little money left over for charitable uses (lines 79-108). Those whom lack of virtue has made unhappy (this Stoic identification of happiness with virtue is an echo of the fourth epistle of the *Essay on Man*) search vainly for the satisfactions of life through money; failing to find what they seek, they die rich and miserable, leaving their unused wealth to hated or unworthy heirs (cf. *Epistle to a Lady*, lines 149-150). The pharisaical cant of the uncharitable, the Bonds and the Heathcotes and the Blunts who would withhold even necessities from the poor on the ground that poverty is an infallible sign of idleness, leads Pope naturally to the specifically Christian (or un-Christian) couplet,

> Yet, to be just to these poor men of pelf,
> Each does but hate his neighbour as himself.

(Lines 109-110)

This hideous perversion of the second great commandment of Christ emphasizes not only the material wretchedness of the poor but the spiritual wretchedness of the uncharitable rich. The couplet marks one of the darkest points in the poem. Pope clearly perceives the emotional distress of those who frantically accumulate and hoard wealth which, in the very nature of things, they cannot enjoy (cf. *Epistle to Burlington*, lines 1-2); and he sees that in their apparent hatred of their fellow men there is a paradoxical but inescapable element of self-loathing. Far from being a sign of God's Grace, material wealth may all too often be the mark of an impoverished spirit; this is an idea which lurks beneath the surface of the whole epistle. Pope is so struck by these anomalies that he attempts to probe the motives which drive men and women so compulsively toward the thing which creates their own spiritual misery:

> Who suffer thus, mere Charity should own,
> Must act on motives pow'rful, tho' unknown.

(Lines 113-114)

51

These motives he finds to be fear (cf. *Im. Hor.*, Ep. i. 1. 67-70), ambition, greed, and (with the re-entry of the Puritan Blunt at line 135) a fanatically self-righteous desire to reform the nation (lines 115-152). The psychological aberrations here presented are close to the inconsistencies which form the theme of the first two Moral Essays: they are self-defeating and contrary to nature, and they are quite inexplicable.

Here Pope effects a transition into a more patently philosophic aspect of the discussion by introducing, as the source of all this madness, the Ruling Passion (lines 153-160; cf. *To Cobham*, lines 174 ff.). At this juncture the argument once again takes on a marked resemblance to that in the *Essay on Man*:

> Hear then the truth: " 'Tis Heav'n each Passion sends,
> "And diff'rent men directs to diff'rent ends.
> "Extremes in Nature equal good produce,
> "Extremes in Man concur to gen'ral use."
>
> (*Epistle to Bathurst*, lines 161-164)

An almost identical statement appears in the second epistle of the *Essay*:

> Extremes in Nature equal ends produce,
> In Man they join to some mysterious use.
>
> (*Essay on Man*, II, 205-206)

The extremes which Pope is discussing here are avarice and extravagance, the two Ruling Passions which form the subjects, respectively, of the *Epistle to Bathurst* and the *Epistle to Burlington*. The point which he emphasizes in *To Bathurst* is that even though the vices of the miser and the prodigal are in themselves wicked and may well create temporary inequities in the distribution of the world's wealth, the wisdom and benevolence of God will turn them ultimately to universal good. (We shall see presently that this does not serve to relieve the individual of his moral and ethical obligations.) God effects this ultimate good in human affairs in much the same way and for much the same reasons that He does it in external nature, a conviction which Pope expresses in a majestic passage compounded almost equally of Genesis (8:22) and Vergil's *Georgics* (i. 1-42):

> Ask we what makes one keep, and one bestow?
> That Pow'ʀ who bids the Ocean ebb and flow,
> Bids seed-time, harvest, equal course maintain,
> Thro' reconcil'd extremes of drought and rain,
> Builds Life on Death, on Change Duration founds,
> And gives th' eternal wheels to know their rounds.

(*Epistle to Bathurst*, lines 165-170)

This doctrine Pope has already established as his own point of view, in opposition to the more cynical opinions of Lord Bathurst, near the beginning of the poem (lines 1-14). Bathurst, we are told, believes that riches, and man's pellmell scramble to acquire them, are nothing but a huge, cosmic joke perpetrated by the powers of heaven for their particular amusement. Pope states as his own opinion, on the other hand, that when gold was first wrested from its underground hiding place,

> Then careful Heav'n supply'd two sorts of Men,
> To squander These, and Those to hide agen.

(Lines 13-14)

Throughout the epistle Pope is making the very point which he emphasizes in the *Essay on Man* (I, 151-160), that extremes are to be expected in mankind as in external nature but that

53

God ("careful Heav'n") is aware of the situation and will manipulate it to His own ends. And "careful Heav'n" is an important phrase to notice here, for it contains the germ of all that Pope is saying about God not only in the *Epistle to Bathurst* but wherever he refers to God's purposes in his poetry. Indeed, the specific problem of the hoarders and wasters Pope had broached to Joseph Spence as early as May 1730, nearly three years before the publication of the *Epistle to Bathurst*:

> As to yᵉ General Design of Providence yᵉ two extremes of a Vice, serve like two opposite biasses to keep up yᵉ Ballance of things. Avarice, lays up (wᵗ wᵈ be hurtful;) Prodigality, scatters abroad (wᵗ may be useful in other hands:) The middle yᵉ point for Virtue. . . .[41]

In all these statements it is clear that Pope is venturing once more upon several of his favorite themes: the Ruling Passion, the tendency to go to extremes, the Golden Mean between those extremes, and God's management of the extremes to the universal good of all mankind. These ideas of Pope's, from the time of Crousaz onward, have been sometimes misinterpreted as evidence that Pope cherished a necessitarian or deterministic attitude toward human destiny. Wasserman calls attention to Courthope's "almost perverse misreading" of the *Epistle to Bathurst* and effectually refutes Courthope's charge that Pope is at one moment attacking the extreme economic vices and at the next contradicting himself by asserting that they are part of God's universal plan.[42] With regard to the *Epistle to Bathurst*, the conventional argument against Pope runs somewhat as follows: according to Pope's own statement, the Ruling Passion, which drives

---

41 "Pope at Work," p. 50.
42 Wasserman, pp. 33-40. Courthope's statement may be found at EC. 121.

men to such extremes as profusion and avarice, is ordained by Heaven and serves God's long-range purposes for the human race, and the same may be said for all the evil which exists in the world; if, therefore, a man feels impelled to be a spendthrift or a miser, this impulse has been implanted in him by God; it is useless to resist such an impulse, for to do so would be to frustrate God's purposes and, indeed, to attempt the impossible; Mandeville was right: private vices are public benefits, and the obvious inference to be drawn from Pope's words is that the greater and more numerous the individual vices, the greater and more numerous the universal benefits; Pope is therefore inconsistent in attacking the very extremes which he holds in the next breath to be part of the Divine Plan.

So runs the argument: Pope is committed to both determinism and libertine naturalism; and he is self-contradictory as well. The first of these objections, as voiced by Crousaz and later by Johnson, we have already noticed in the analysis of the *Epistle to Cobham*: it fails to take account of the role of reason in determining men's actions and in assigning the direction which the Ruling Passion will take. The second objection, that Pope is contradicting himself by condemning what he regards as divinely ordained, fails to distinguish between the individual and the whole. We are a fallen race inhabiting a fallen world; opportunities for vicious, oppressive, and irrational behavior leap at us from every side. So much Pope has made evident from the very beginning of the poem. Are we then to conclude from this sad state of affairs that God is wicked and that He has all along intended that we should be wicked too? To do so is to commit the error described by Soame Jenyns:

Our difficulties arise from our forgetting how many difficulties Omnipotence has to contend with: in the present instance it is obliged either to afflict innocence or be the cause of wickedness; it plainly has no other option.[43]

Omnipotence nevertheless has managed to surmount these difficulties by taking evil as He finds it and turning it, in the long run, to the service of good. The greatest example of His doing so is the Redemption of man through Christ, whereby the greatest evil ever to befall God's Creation, the disobedience and fall of man, has been turned correspondingly to the greatest good. Dante's great poem is called a comedy because of the joyous promise with which Dante the traveler emerges from a state of sin into a state of grace; and the conclusion of *Paradise Lost*, by the same token, is full of hope. And the process, as Pope makes perfectly clear in the *Essay on Man*, is still going on: God is still, in some mysterious fashion unknown to us, bringing good out of evil. The example given in the *Epistle to Bathurst* is that God redresses the balance between the two extremes of parsimony and profusion and sees to it that the money so sinfully misused by individual misers and prodigals ultimately finds its way to the general good. This is the function of Dame Fortune as Dante makes Vergil explain it in the *Inferno*:

> That king whose perfect wisdom transcends all,
>   made the heavens and posted angels on them
>   to guide the eternal light that it might fall
>
> from every sphere to every sphere the same.
>   He made earth's splendors by a like decree
>   and posted as their minister this high Dame,
>
> the Lady of Permutations. All earth's gear
>   she changes from nation to nation, from house to house,
>   in changeless change through every turning year.[44]

(*Inferno*, vii, 73-81)

---

43 Quoted in Arthur O. Lovejoy, *The Great Chain of Being* (New York: Harper and Brothers, 1960), p. 210.

44 Dante Alighieri, *The Inferno*, trans. John Ciardi (New York: New American Library, 1954), p. 74.

This is Pope's argument that the same Divine Benevolence
which provides for an equitable distribution of His cosmic
gifts to man (lines 165-170) also provides for an equitable
distribution of such lesser blessings as money—but only when
the time, in His total scheme of things, is ripe. And when
Dante uses the term *Fortune*, he intends it to be understood
as Divine Providence, with no suggestion of determinism or
the abridgment of individual free will (cf. *De Monarchia*,
XII, 70).[45]

Nevertheless, it does not follow from this that man should
actively pursue evil in order that God may bring good out
of it; it does not follow that man should allow himself the
easy luxury of running to extremes merely because God
has shown Himself willing to reconcile and redeem those
extremes when they do occur. As Wasserman expresses it,
". . . the moral duty of the individual man is to strive to
fulfill the final end for which he was created, regardless of
God's economy of the whole."[46] The individual must ever
strive to observe the dictates of reason and thereby to avoid
extremes. If he succeeds, well and good. If he fails, he may
bring tragedy to himself and others, and he is assuredly a
fool; but, viewing the matter *sub specie aeternitatis*, those
who have faith may rest assured that through God's goodness
the human race, though not necessarily the individual, will
somehow be the better for it. Warburton summarizes Pope's
position in a commentary on the passage beginning at line
153 (line 151 in the 1751 edition):

'Tis HEAVEN itself that gives the *ruling* Passion,
and thereby directs different men to different ends:
But these being exerted through the ministry of

---

45 There was a time, however, when Dante, like Pope, was accused of
denying free will to man, but see the note to Ciardi's translation of
the *Inferno*, p. 77.
46 Wasserman, p. 35.

NATURE (of whom the great *Bacon* truly observes, *modum tenere nescia est*, Aug. Scient. 1. ii. c. 13) they are very apt to run into extremes: To correct which, Heaven, at the same time, added the moderatrix *Reason*; not to take the *ruling Passion* out of the the hands and ministry of *Nature*, but to restrain and rectify its irregular impulses (See *Essay*, Ep. ii, v. 151, & *seq.*) and what extremes after this, remained uncorrected . . . the divine artist himself has, in his heavenly skill and bounty, set to rights; by so ordering, that these of the *moral*, like those of the natural world, should, even by the very means of their contrariety and diversity, concur to defeat the malignity of one another: [quotes lines 163-164]. For as the various seasons of the year are supported and sustained by the reconciled extremes of Wet and Dry, Cold and Heat; so all the *orders* and *degrees* of civil life are kept up by *Avarice* and *Profusion, Selfishness* and *Vanity*. The Miser being but the Steward of the Prodigal; and only so much the more backward as the other is violent and precipitate: [quotes lines 175-176].[47]

Thus does "careful Heav'n" remedy the follies and vices of an imperfect world. If, then, Pope condemns the misers for withholding money which might be useful, only to declare later on that such men are really "backward stewards for the poor" (line 174), he is making two statements which are not contradictory but complementary: stinginess is wicked and inexcusable in the individual, but God will not allow it to leave a permanent scar on His Creation. The miser's money will be put to use in the fullness of God's time. Extravagance, the opposite extreme, is equally irrational, but it serves to balance the scales in God's total economy; so much is made clear in lines 171-178.

As examples of these two extremes Pope presents the sketches of the niggardly Cotta and his wastrel son. The

---

47 Warburton, pp. 235-236.

old man himself is portrayed in a series of telling paradoxes. He is, of course, rich, but he lives like a pauper. His similarity to Dryden's "Shimei" shows that he is probably a Whig and a Puritan (see line 182 and notes 74 and 110), as does the ironic question in line 188 ("And who would take the Poor from Providence?"), which echoes the smug cruelty of Bond, Heathcote, and Blunt (lines 102-106). Pope's intention, furthermore, is made even clearer by the fact that the remark given to Heathcote (lines 103-104) was originally assigned to this same Cotta in the Huntington manuscripts (cf. note 47); the easy transferral of the lines from Cotta to Heathcote shows well enough that in Pope's mind all four were grouped together as examples of Puritan stinginess. But this stinginess, with its ascetic manner of living, Pope ironically equates with the austerity of the Carthusian monks (line 189), who on most days of the year (Sundays and feast days excepted) take only one meal, each monk in the solitude of his own cell, and who for almost nine centuries have eaten no meat whatever. The Carthusians live thus from motives of dedicated piety; Cotta does it from sheer parsimony. The Carthusians perform notable acts of charity; but Cotta, although he lives like them, dispenses no such charity from his "unop'ning door" (line 196). It is characteristic of Pope's subtle allusiveness that a fleeting reference, buried in a single line ("Like some lone Chartreux stands the good old Hall"), is capable of creating such a wealth of ironic suggestion, raising questions which bear a significance not only ethical but sectarian as well. Perhaps without realizing it, Pope has come very close here to one of the great controversies which have always divided Catholic and Protestant Christians, the problem of justification; and the problem is implied throughout the poem.

Cotta himself, then, cannot enjoy his riches, for what he denies others he denies also to himself:

His court with nettles, moats with cresses stor'd,
With soups unbought and sallads bless'd his board.

(Lines 183-184)

As Pope pointedly remarks in a note to these lines, there is a reminiscence here of Vergil, *Georgics* iv. 133: "dapibus mensas onerabat inemptis" ("he loaded his table with unbought delicacies"). This allusion, too, is fraught with irony, for the passage is taken from Vergil's well-known description of the old Corycian gardener, who through loving care and plain hard work has transformed a barren, rocky plot of ground into a little paradise of fruits and vegetables and flowers. These simple delicacies are "unbought" not because the Corycian is rich and niggardly but because he is a poor man, cast upon his own resources, who has achieved through fruitful labor a high degree of happiness and peace of mind: his contentment rivals the wealth of kings ("regum aequabat opes animis," line 132). He is, in his modest way, productive; Cotta, for all his wealth, is sterile. This contrast between fruitfulness and sterility, a basic theme of both the *Epistle to Bathurst* and the *Epistle to Burlington*, gains added significance later in the poem, when Cotta himself is compared with the Man of Ross. And the contrast is further strengthened when this admittedly ironic echo of the *Georgics* is set against such seriously georgic passages as the statement in lines 165-170 and the lines recounting the public works of the Man of Ross (lines 249-258). Neither of these latter passages is so specific an allusion to Vergil as is the Cotta couplet, but there is about them an air of genuinely creative, almost cosmic, beneficence (even in Pope's way of describing the modest achievements of the Man of Ross) which recalls Vergil's invocation of the Roman agricultural deities and of the emperor Augustus himself (*Georgics* i. 1-42). Cotta is equally capable of the munificence of these gods—or, for that matter, of the Carthusian monks—but his irrational

60

parsimony forbids it. The Corycian swain is in some sense a proto-Carthusian; and, by bringing the two together in similar patterns of irony, Pope is showing that men like Cotta stand convicted of abject selfishness by any civilized standards, pagan or Christian. In the face of every injunction to charity, hospitality, and public usefulness, Cotta holds himself coldly aloof from all the world, while "his gaunt mastiff growling at the gate" (line 197) keeps the rest of the world away from him.

At the opposite pole from old Cotta is his spendthrift son, who noted well his father's miserly behavior "And then mistook reverse of wrong for right" (line 200). Pope has already established his conviction that the two extremes will ultimately be balanced out in God's total economy of the universe; from the individual standpoint, however, they cannot directly counteract each other, and the one extreme is just as wicked as the other. Pope was to say the same thing in another poem a year and a half later:

> 'Tis yet in vain, I own, to make a pother
> About one vice, and fall into the other:
> Between Excess and Famine lies a mean;
> Plain, but not sordid; tho' not splendid, clean.

> (*Im. Hor.*, Sat. ii. 2. 45-48)

Dante describes a similar situation in the *Purgatorio*, where the poet Statius has just completed five hundred years of penance for prodigality, a penance which he has performed at the cornice of the opposite sin, avarice (Cornice V):

> "For when the opposite of a sin, as here,
>   is as blameworthy as the sin itself,
>   both lose their growth together and turn sere.

> If, then, I lay so long in my distress

61

among the Avaricious where they weep,
it was to purge the opposite excess."[48]

(*Purgatorio*, xxii, 49-54)

Apart from the question of penance, with which Pope is not concerned here, this is young Cotta's case exactly: the son is trying to eradicate the sins of the father by going to the opposite extreme. Where the father denied hospitality altogether, the son pours it forth in "slaughtered hecatombs [and] floods of wine" (line 203). Where the father gave to no one, the son squanders his entire substance to finance a war. And where the father gave little sign of religious feeling in any direction, the Puritan "enthusiasm" of the son extends to rioting in the streets and burning the Pope of Rome in effigy. Warburton points out in his commentary that Cotta and his son are examples of the two opposite Ruling Passions which the poem has been describing.[49] Like Dante in both the *Inferno* and the *Purgatorio*, Pope has placed the hoarders and the wasters side by side as opposite and mutually antagonistic extremes; but in Pope's world view, as in Dante's, these extremes contribute only to the moral downfall of the individuals themselves. They do not invalidate God's wisdom in the Creation.

The flagrant irrationality of these two extremes is now offset by a return to sense (lines 219-220); and Bathurst himself is invoked, as a sort of muse of common sense, to teach by his own example the wisdom of the Golden Mean (lines 227-228). If a man of wealth is to accomplish this great objective, he must exercise rare judgment in matters of privilege and responsibility; he must manage his resources wisely ("Œconomy") while at the same time living in a manner appropriate to his station in life ("Magnificence"),

---

48 Dante Alighieri, *The Purgatorio*, trans. John Ciardi (New York: New American Library, 1961), p. 226.
49 Warburton, pp. 238-239.

and he must not allow the splendor of his own domestic arrangements to blind him to the needs of others (lines 223-225). This balance the wealthy nobility can achieve if they will; but even the rich and noble must yield to John Kyrle, the humble Man of Ross, who dispenses charity at every hand on a modest income of five hundred pounds a year (lines 249-280). This story was too much for Samuel Johnson, who exclaimed of the Man of Ross, "Wonders are willingly told and willingly heard."[50] Johnson, in his intense practicality, thought that Pope had vitiated the whole moral force of the *exemplum* by making it sound incredible, and he felt constrained to remark on his own initiative that Kyrle had apparently received assistance in his charities from people of greater wealth than he. "Narrations of romantick and impracticable virtue will be read with wonder," Johnson goes on, "but that which is unattainable is recommended in vain; that good may be endeavoured, it must be shown to be possible."

What Johnson says is true; yet Pope has made it clear that he has introduced the Man of Ross in order to shame the uncharitable rich and even to show charitable men like Bathurst that this indispensable part of the Christian life is not restricted to the wealthy (lines 249, 281-282). In a letter to Jacob Tonson dated June 7, 1732, Pope says of the Man of Ross,

> My motive in singling out this man was twofold. First to distinguish Real and solid worth from showish or plausible expense, and virtue from vanity; and secondly to humble the pride of greater men, by an opposition of one so obscure and so distant from all yᵉ sphere of public glory—this proud town. To send you any of the particular verses will be much to the prejudice of the whole, which if it has any Beauty

---

50 Johnson, VIII, 292.

derives it from the manner in which it is Placed as y^e
*contras*TE (as ye Painters call it) in which it stands
with ye pompous figures of famous or rich or high
born men.[51]

Pope is not speaking, then, as Johnson assumes, to those
who have five hundred pounds a year. He is speaking primarily to the really rich and attempting to demonstrate that
what is possible for the Man of Ross is surely possible for
them.

Assuming that Pope knew of the help which the Man
of Ross received in his charities, we still cannot be absolutely
certain whether he suppressed the information because he
felt that he could not fit it into his poem or because he feared
that he might weaken his argument. The latter reason is
the more likely, for Pope admitted to Tonson in the same
letter that "a small exaggeration" must be allowed him as
a poet:

If any man shall ever happen to endeavour to emulate
the Man of Ross, 'twill be no manner of harm if I
make him think he was something more charitable
and more Beneficent than really he was, for so much
more good it w^{ld} put the imitator upon doing. . . .

At any rate, it is undeniable that Pope is trying very hard in
this episode to emphasize a point—but the point is not
only that charity is possible for rich and poor alike but that,
on whatever financial terms charity is undertaken, it is glorious.
The Christian deeds of the Man of Ross cannot even ap-
proximate those of the Earl of Burlington in the fourth
Moral Essay (lines 191-204), but their real significance lies
in the loving Christian spirit in which they are undertaken.
The widow's mite, offered in a true spirit of charity, puts
to shame the hoarded millions of the miser or the squandered

---

51 EC, 529; *Corr*, III, 290.

millions of the profligate; and it is the tremendous power of charity as a spiritual force, however humble its origin, that Pope is seeking to dramatize in the Man of Ross. For this reason he intentionally employs the language of epic hyperbole in speaking of Kyrle's achievements, achievements which deserve to be ranked with the beneficence of a deity, Christian or otherwise, toward the human race. Kyrle laid out a shady walk, about a mile and a half long, on the top of a hill overlooking the River Wye, but Pope glorifies the deed by saying that the Man of Ross cooled the "sultry brow" of a mountain, much as one of the Roman agricultural gods invoked by Vergil (*Georgics* i. 1-42) might have done. Kyrle arranged for the construction of a small waterwork which brought running water to the town of Ross, but Pope again glorifies the act by associating it with the great act of Moses in commanding water to flow out of dry rock (Exodus 17:6).[52] Such altruism is far removed from the wasteful ostentation of Timon, whose pond is an ocean (*Epistle to Burlington*, line 106); it represents, on the contrary, a fruitful expenditure of money, and in his eagerness to commend these examples of Christian charity Pope symbolically enlarges them to match the achievements of a Moses or a Caesar Augustus.

The zeal for charity which induced Pope to glorify the deeds of the Man of Ross has led him, however, into some rather ineffective poetry. His description of Kyrle's shady walk as cooling the sultry brow of a mountain, as though the mountain itself were suffering from the heat, is a far-fetched and inorganic conceit; and to equate the irrigation project at Ross with the miracles of Moses is to overstate the case. A few lines further on, moreover, Pope's enthusiasm for Kyrle's charities traps him into a somewhat complacent observation on the almshouse which Kyrle supports, "Where Age and Want sit smiling at the gate" (lines 265-266). By

---

52 EC, 150.

twentieth-century standards, at least, Pope's age seems to have been quite insensitive to the affront to human dignity implied in statements of this kind. Still, for the twentieth century to sit in pious judgment on the eighteenth in matters of social responsibility is to indulge in the luxury of hindsight (the subject is highly complex), and it must be admitted that the episode of the Man of Ross, however awkwardly sentimental it may appear, is a true story and that it serves to dramatize charity as a Christian duty incumbent upon all who profess to follow the teachings of the Gospels. Pope is trying to show that all Christians, regardless of their means or their sectarian preferences, must be doers of the word and not hearers only.

Indeed, the contrast which Pope has been emphasizing between the miserly and the charitable immediately suggests the Parable of the Sheep and the Goats in the Gospel according to Saint Matthew (25:31-46), and though Pope's own *exemplum* may not be a specific vision of the Last Judgment, it can be construed in a very real sense as a parable of separation. But even the mere act of separation, upon the terms which Pope implies, has within it the hallmark of an apocalypse. The Cottas, the Bonds, the Heathcotes, and the Blunts will huddle trembling at the left side of the Throne; but the Man of Ross, and all others like him, will be set at the King's right hand to inherit the Kingdom prepared for them from the foundation of the world and to hear the words, "Verily I say unto you, inasmuch as ye have ministered unto one of the least of these my brethren, ye have ministered unto me." Although it is hard to believe that these words may not have flashed across Pope's mind as he pondered the tale of the Man of Ross, the fact remains that he did not wish to carry the poem this far into Christian eschatology, and he therefore does not press the implication. At the same time, by his other contrast, that between the charity of the Man of Ross and the squanderings of young Cotta, Pope emphasizes the classical coloring of the epistle by bringing in a third element, implying that the Man of Ross is not exactly opposite to either of the Cottas but represents a Golden Mean between them. Pope's vision, in the final reckoning, is not polar but triangular.

Several illustrations of the abuse of money now follow in the form of swiftly delineated satiric portraits. There is the miserly Hopkins, whose ugly and pretentious monument (cf. notes 94 and 95) contrasts sharply with the brief entry in the parish register commemorating the Man of Ross (lines 283-298). There is the wastrel Villiers, second Duke of Buckingham (Dryden's "Zimri"), who died, according to Pope, in miserable poverty (cf. note 97). There is the rich and niggardly Cutler (cf. note 100), who supposedly bestowed his daughter upon an unworthy stranger rather than provide her with a dowry (lines 315-334). From these portraits Pope now moves toward the conclusion of his poem with a puzzling transition. He has pushed his argument to the point where very little of a purely ethical nature remains to be said, but the death of Cutler inevitably raises the more solemn question of Heaven and Hell and the Last Judgment: "Say for such worth are other worlds prepar'd?" (line 335). But having posed this ironic question, Pope evades its implications; and in doing so he indicates his unwillingness to pursue the matter from ethics into theology. It is as though he felt his discussion of this world trembling on the brink of the next, and he therefore brings himself up short with a tacit admission of his inability or his unwillingness to explore the eschatological aspects of the problem any further. Instead he reverts to his customary satiric technique of providing an *exemplum*, introducing it with the rather feeble excuse that Bathurst has grown weary of abstractions (lines 337-338 and note 103).

If the story of the Man of Ross suggests the Parable of the Sheep and the Goats, the sordid tale of Sir Balaam is strongly reminiscent of the Book of Job. But Pope is inverting the story of Job, for in recounting the Balaam episode his purpose is to show the corrupting influence of riches, rather than the salutary effects of poverty or the fortitude with which adversity may conceivably be endured. Still, it is important to remember that Pope has already implied the sterility of riches and their inability to produce any effect, either good or bad, without human assistance. What emerges from the story of Sir Balaam, then, is another problem in fundamental human ethics, the curious circumstance that just as alcohol can addict only the addictable, riches can corrupt only the corruptible. Riches have not corrupted Lord Bathurst, nor have they corrupted Burlington, the nobleman addressed in the fourth Moral Essay. Sir Balaam, however, is plainly vulnerable. In the first place, his residence next to the Monument, with its Puritan-inspired inscription blaming the London fire of 1666 on the Roman Catholics (cf. line 340 and note 104), marks him a Puritan and a Whig and thus, according to Pope, a scoundrel in money matters. From this there follows a second point, that his only virtues are the economic qualities glorified by Calvin, qualities which Pope describes (lines 341-344) with a significant lack of enthusiasm. Despite his superficial piety, Balaam's soul lies hidden in his purse; he is stingy, avaricious, and shrewd, in the Puritan manner which has been emphasized throughout the poem in the portraits of Cotta and the others (note especially lines 347-348). Third, the very name Balaam, as Professor Wasserman has shown, was traditionally associated in the New Testament and by later Scriptural commentators with avarice and financial chicanery.[53] Deeply ingrained, therefore, within Balaam's very soul is a fundamental weakness which is already apparent to an astute

---

53 Wasserman, pp. 45-46.

observer and which awaits only its due season to blossom into full-blown evil. As Dryden expresses it in a poem which Pope has already echoed several times in this epistle,

> But when to sin our biassed nature leans,
> The careful Devil is still at hand with means.

(Absalom and Achitophel, lines 79-80)

The Devil, in other words, knows his own. When Pope remarks that

> The Devil was piqu'd such saintship to behold,
> And long'd to tempt him like good Job of old

(Lines 349-350)

the irony makes it clear that the Devil has spotted an easy mark, that there is no "saintship" here save the Puritans' smug and canting application of the word to themselves, that Balaam will be led with ridiculous ease from smaller evils into greater ones as his financial capacities increase, that whatever relationship may exist between Balaam and good Job of old lies not in their similarity but in their oppositeness. Pope's technique in the Balaam episode is, in this sense, that of the mock-epic: he achieves a devastating incongruity by equating a foolish or vicious "hero" with the truly wise and virtuous hero of ancient story, except that in this instance the underlying framework is not classical but Scriptural. As Colley Cibber, in The Dunciad, is a distorted Aeneas, crowned king not of Rome but of Dullness, so Balaam is a distorted Job, not strengthened through hardship but corrupted by prosperity.

The fact that the Devil now "tempts by making rich, not making poor" (line 352) is the crowning, almost Faustian, irony of the Balaam episode. Balaam is indeed made rich—

69

first through a stroke of sheer luck (or the "providence" of Satan), later through what is for Pope a characteristic bit of Puritan chicanery (lines 353-364)—and riches are his undoing. Like Danaë in the embrace of Zeus, he is possessed by the Devil in a shower of gold (lines 371-374). Like Faustus (and by interweaving Faustus, Job, and Danaë, Pope is again mingling Christian and classical elements as he has been doing throughout the poem) he is provided by the Devil with every advantage of material wealth; and, like Faustus, he quickly becomes irreverent and proud. He receives stolen property—in Pope's hyperbolic presentation it is the famous Pitt diamond (cf. note 108)—and then steals it in his turn, sanctimoniously vowing to make amends in church for his peculations (lines 365-368). But this twinge of conscience soon wears off, and Balaam comes to neglect even the lip service which he had paid, in his former moderate circumstances, to his Puritan faith. His newly acquired wealth he ascribes to his own unaided efforts, conveniently forgetting the Puritan belief that material prosperity comes from Divine Providence (lines 375-378). He is no longer even nominally devout; working on Sunday mornings and driving in St. James's Park, Balaam the pseudo-Puritan has become Balaam the pseudo-aristocrat.

But the Devil, to whom Balaam has in effect sold his soul, has already begun to collect his due, and disaster now follows hard upon disaster. His wife and son perish, and his daughter becomes a complete disgrace. His second wife, a worthless gold-digger and social climber, piles up such heavy gambling debts that he is forced to commit an act of treason to pay them, and thus Pope reinforces his earlier reminiscence of Aristotle's *Ethics* in lumping together the sins of avarice, usury, speculation, prostitution, and gambling under the general category of base gain. Balaam is convicted of treason and hanged. His soul is instantly snatched up by

the Devil, and all the material gains for which he bartered
it are forfeit to the crown:

> The Devil and the King divide the prize,
> And sad Sir Balaam curses God and dies.

(Lines 401-402)

"The careful Devil" has found the chink in the Puritan's
moral armor and has turned the discovery to his own advantage. Where Job remained steadfast in adversity, Balaam
crumbles in prosperity. Where all that Job lost was restored
to him, all that Balaam gained reverts to the Crown, to be
used for purposes of good (Pope would doubtless have us
assume) in the fullness of God's time. Where Job stood high
in the favor of God, Balaam is condemned to eternal fire.
It is therefore fitting that Balaam's last words, and the last
words of Pope to the reader, should be an echo of the
blasphemies suggested to Job by his wife and indignantly
repudiated:

> Then said his wife unto him, Dost thou still
> retain thine integrity? curse God and die. But
> he said unto her, Thou speakest as one of the
> foolish women speaketh. What? shall we receive
> good at the hand of God, and shall we not
> receive evil? In all this did not Job sin
> with his lips.

(Job 2:9-10)

In the same way, Balaam can have no legitimate complaint.
He has received good, according to his definition of it, at
the hand of Satan, and he has also received evil. Both
hoarder and spender by turns, he has plumbed the depths of
immorality in the acquisition and the use of riches, and the
outcome is that he must pay the price of Faustus and of all
who abuse and manipulate the world's wealth from avaricious

71

motives. Although he is not so miserly as Cotta or so prodigal as Cotta's son, he combines within himself the irrational extremes which Pope has intentionally isolated in the two Cottas, the extremes which Pope is attacking throughout this long and complex poem on the use of riches. Like all misers and prodigals, Balaam has obeyed the teachings of the Devil, and the implied nature of his final fate shows clearly that Pope, in spite of himself, has once again drawn very close to the borders of Christian eschatology.

E P I S T L E   I V

To Richard Boyle,
Earl of Burlington

The *Epistle to Burlington* was the earliest of Pope's Moral Essays in point of publication, appearing for the first time in December 1731. A footnote attributed to Pope (cf. line 23) indicates that the poem was intended in part as a tribute to two published works on architecture in which Burlington had at least a considerable share: *The Designs of Inigo Jones, consisting of Plans and Elevations for Public and Private Buildings*,[54] published in 1727 under the name of Burlington's favorite architect, William Kent (1684-1748);[55] and *Fabbriche Antiche disegnate da Andrea Palladio Vicentino*, published in 1730 under the name of Burlington himself. The text of Pope's epistle was to have appeared in a projected second volume of the latter work, but the second volume was never published.[56]

Richard Boyle (1695-1753), third Earl of Burlington and fourth Earl of Cork, was a remarkable person. As a youth he had lived for several years in Italy, where he developed a passion for the symmetrical style of Andrea Palladio (1518-1580), the great Venetian architect, and he devoted his life to a systematic study of Palladio and his influence on European taste. Burlington became an amateur architect in his own right, and was probably the designer of the alterations made about 1716 to his celebrated town residence, Burlington House, Piccadilly. Here he entertained Pope, Gay, Handel, and

---

54 These drawings were probably not by Jones but by his pupil John Webb; cf. B. Sprague Allen, *Tides in English Taste*, 2 vols. (Cambridge, Mass.: Harvard University Press, 1937), I, 58.

55 A rather fulsome tribute to Kent can be found in John Gay's *Epistle to the Right Honourable Paul Methuen, Esq.*, line 53-74. Probably both Gay and Burlington overrated Kent's abilities as an architect.

56 TE, xxiv-xxv.

other notable figures of the period; and Gay, to whom Burlington was exceptionally generous, wrote of Burlington House as one of the showplaces of London:

> Yet *Burlington*'s fair palace still remains;
> Beauty within, without proportion reigns.
> Beneath his eye declining art revives,
> The wall with animated pictures lives;
> There *Hendel* strikes the strings, the melting strain
> Transports the soul, and thrills through ev'ry vein;
> There oft' I enter (but with cleaner shoes)
> For *Burlington*'s belov'd by ev'ry Muse.

(Trivia, II, 493-500)

Burlington House seems to have been regarded by some as rather overdecorated (if it was, Pope chooses to ignore the fact), and that its beauties did not meet with unmitigated acclaim is shown by Hogarth's satirical print "Taste of the Town," in which the earl's architectural ideas are made the butt of some derision. In 1854 Burlington House was acquired in all its splendor by the British Government, and it now houses the Royal Society, the Linnean Society, and the Society of Antiquaries.

Between 1730 and 1736 Burlington designed and built a new villa on his suburban estate at Chiswick, rather ineptly modeled after Palladio's Villa Rotonda at Vicenza. Concerning Pope's *al fresco* visits at Chiswick House, Gay has left the following pleasant observation:

> While you, my Lord, bid stately piles ascend,
> Or in your *Chiswick* bow'rs enjoy your friend;
> Where *Pope* unloads the boughs within his reach,
> Of purple vine, blue plumb, and blushing peach;
> I journey far. . . .

("An Epistle to the Right Honourable
the Earl of Burlington: A Journey
to Exeter," lines 1-5)

Aside from his entertainment and support of the poets of
the day, Burlington was at various times patron of the
philosopher Berkeley, host and patron to the composer Handel,
and a director of the Royal Academy of Music for the per-
formance of Handel's compositions. He designed many other
buildings besides his own, though probably not without professional assistance, and he contributed large sums of money
to the government for the creation of public buildings, bridges,
and roads; indeed, he very nearly bankrupted himself in this
way. It will be noted that, although Pope says little of Burlington's abilities as an architect, he gives the earl full meed
of praise for his generous encouragement of public works
(lines 191-204).[57]

It is likely that the influence of Burlington's Palladian
tastes did much to discourage the popularity in England of
such monstrous—and monstrously expensive—baroque piles
as those designed by Vanbrugh for the Duke of Marlborough at Blenheim and George Bubb Dodington at Eastbury in Dorsetshire. Spence reports that "Lord Burlington
was so much for Palladio that he used to run down Michael
Angelo";[58] and the earl is said to have thrown up his hands
in horror at his first glimpse of Christopher Wren's new
Saint Paul's in London. At any rate, neither the baroque nor
the rococo style gained as much headway in eighteenth-century England as on the Continent, but in the simplicity and
symmetry of Georgian architecture the influence of Palladio
is clearly at work. For this development Burlington probably
deserves some credit, and it is therefore not surprising that
simplicity and good taste are the keynotes of the epistle which
Pope addresses to his lordship. In fact, the poem is in great
measure an application to architecture and landscaping—

---

57 Pope praises Burlington again in the notes to *Dunciad* (A), III,
323-324.
58 P. 106.

subjects on which Pope himself, though an amateur, was something of an authority—of some basic principles laid down in his youthful *Essay on Criticism*. Thus, it is primarily Horatian in its esthetic, in its objection to vulgar and ostentatious display, and in its espousal of the basic principles of naturalness and good taste.

Closely related to these attitudes is the matter of riches, the proper use of which receives extensive discussion in the *Epistle to Bathurst*. In the present poem Pope confines his attack to what Thorstein Veblen was later to call conspicuous consumption, to pointless exhibitions of wealth for its own sake, to the enormous mansions and the artificial gardens which serve primarily to gratify the vanity of their owners by demonstrating a limitless ability to spend money. Veblen writes in Chapter 4 of *The Theory of the Leisure Class*, "Throughout the entire evolution of conspicuous expenditure . . . runs the obvious implication that in order to effectually mend the consumer's good fame it must be an expenditure of superfluities. In order to be reputable it must be wasteful."[59] The man who constructs house and garden primarily to feed his vanity (such a man is Timon in the present poem) must obviously construct something far in excess of what is physically necessary to sustain life. But the trouble is that in a man whose vanity outstrips his taste the physically superfluous, for which there is some excuse, quickly turns into the esthetically superfluous—and for this there can be no excuse at all. Pope heartily disliked the esthetically superfluous—all things gratuitously sumptuous, gratuitously decorative, gratuitously formal; and there is scarcely a line of his own poetry on which such charges can honestly and meaningfully be laid. In this disdain for what does not originate naturally and clearly from the exigencies of a given

---

59 Thorstein Veblen, *The Theory of the Leisure Class* (New York: New American Library, 1953), p. 77.

situation, he anticipates, generally speaking, much that we now take for granted in twentieth-century poetic and architectural theory. In architecture, for example, he prized the unobtrusive and the functional (*Epistle to Burlington,* lines 179-180); in landscaping he disliked the artificial and unnecessary formalism of Dutch and French gardens and preferred instead the kind of grounds which blend naturally with their surroundings while still giving the sense of human control and discipline within an esthetic medium (lines 57-64). This he sums up in his Argument to the *Epistle to Burlington,* declaring that in architecture and landscaping gardening "all must be adapted to the genius and use of the place, and the beauties not forced into it, but resulting from it"; and he had already said as much to Spence in 1729.[60] In erecting a house, in other words, one must bear in mind the use to which the building will be put; in designing a garden, one must exploit as much as possible the characteristic beauty of the surrounding countryside, "the genius of the place," so that the garden forms a harmonious part of a larger whole. English buildings, like those of ancient Rome, must be "glorious, not profuse" (line 23), and the heavy flummery of eighteenth-century imitations of baroque must give way to the severe and imposing simplicity of classical Rome. It is in this thoroughly Horatian vein that Pope remarked to Spence, "Arts are taken from nature; and after a thousand vain efforts for improvements, are best when they return to their first simplicity."[61]

This is the lesson which Burlington's devotion to Palladio has taught the English (lines 23-24), and it cannot be invalidated (Pope continues) by tasteless and ignorant imitators who follow Burlington's rules only by rote, "And of one beauty many blunders make" (line 28). Something is

---

60 Spence, p. 12.
61 Spence, pp. 11-12.

needed above the desire to emulate an earl or the mere willingness to spend money and to show the world that one has it to spend. Taste is needed, the ability not only to follow rules but to understand them and to apply them intelligently to a given architectural problem. And, even more than taste, sense is necessary: "Good Sense, which only is the gift of Heav'n" (line 43). Good sense, which cannot be acquired by imitation but must be developed from within, is the faculty which restrains man's presumptuous lust for pomp and display, dictates unerringly what is appropriate to a given situation, and makes possible an understanding of the total effect created by a building or a garden upon the observer. Good sense, in short, will enable the architect and gardener to follow Nature, for (to borrow a couplet from the *Essay on Criticism*)

> Nature to all things fix'd the limit fit,
> And wisely curb'd proud Man's pretending wit.

> (*Essay on Criticism*, lines 52-53)

To follow Nature, Pope always insists, is the first requirement of any art, whether it be poetry or architecture, for only in this way can the beauty and grandeur of simplicity be attained and the fantastic extremes of overdecoration be avoided. Such an art (to turn again to the *Essay on Criticism*) "Works without show, and without pomp presides" (line 75). Pope's consistency in his preference for the simple and natural over the gaudy extremes of unnecessary adornment is shown by a passage from *The Guardian* No. 173 (September 29, 1713):

> I believe it is no wrong Observation that Persons of Genius, and those who are most capable of Art, are always most fond of Nature, as such are chiefly sensible, that all Art consists in the Imitation and Study of Nature. On the contrary, People of the

common Level of understanding are principally delighted with the little Niceties and Fantastical Operations of Art, and constantly think that *finest* which is least Natural.

And the word *Nature* here, as nearly always in Pope, may be taken to mean the universal principles of order, discipline, harmony, and control which Newton's laws of motion had actually demonstrated as the basis of the entire Creation. People like Addison's Leonora (*Spectator* No. 37), for example, who inadvertently betray themselves as lovers of "the little Niceties and Fantastical Operations of Art," are as plainly defiant of the fundamental order and simplicity of Nature as are the bad poets whom Pope castigates in the *Essay on Criticism*:

> Poets like painters, thus, unskilled to trace
> The naked nature and the living grace,
> With gold and jewels cover every part,
> And hide with ornaments their want of art.

> (*Essay on Criticism*, lines 293-296)

Pope's description of poetry in terms of painting and the jewel box implies his own belief that the esthetic theories which he is discussing are valid for other arts as well. Therefore, those whose houses and gardens betray a delight in meaningless ornamental clutter are at one with the frivolous Leonora and the fantastic poets in doing violence to the principles of Nature.[62]

A related problem created by the use of ornamentation for its own sake is that, by calling too much attention to

---

62 Pope's own garden and grotto belied his principles of simplicity and natural design. The garden was quite formal, and the grotto was decorated, among other things, with bits of shell and broken pieces of looking glass to provide sparkling effects of light. Cf. Allen, *Tides in English Taste*, II, 131-133, and Pope's letter to Edward Blount, June 2, 1725 (*Corr*, II, 296-297).

itself, excessive decoration tends to obscure the total effect. With his characteristically neo-classic fondness for perceiving things in their entirety, rather than piecemeal, Pope everywhere emphasizes the need for a unifying intelligence in every branch of the arts, the need for the kind of genius which can prevent the work of art from falling into mere patchwork brilliance and render it coherent and impressive as a whole. (As applied to human nature, this is the service rendered by the Ruling Passion, as Pope explains in the *Epistle to Cobham*, lines 174 ff. The parallel is by no means accidental.) His advice to critics of literature is highly relevant here:

> In Wit, as Nature, what affects our hearts
> Is not th' exactness of peculiar parts;
> 'Tis not a lip, or eye, we beauty call,
> But the joint force and full result of all.

> (*Essay on Criticism*, lines 243-246)

In the *Epistle to Burlington* this unifying faculty appears not as wit but as sense; it is, in fact, an adjunct of that same "Good Sense, which only is the gift of Heav'n," which we have already noticed at line 43 of the epistle. As wit, in the poet, is his ability to fuse random and fragmentary thoughts or a limited personal experience into universally valid statements about life, so good sense, in the architect, enables him to draw together the details of his structure into a coherent and functional whole—a whole which in much the same way transcends the sum of its parts. Pope, as usual, puts it more succinctly:

> Still follow Sense, of ev'ry Art the Soul,
> Parts answ'ring parts shall slide into a whole.

> (*Epistle to Burlington*, lines 65-66)

If good sense is allowed full reign, unity and wholeness will follow, in due course, with the almost machine-like inevitability suggested by the verb *slide*.[63] In this connection, Warburton's note to line 66 is of great interest:

> [The parts] shall not be *forced*, but *go of themselves;* as if both the parts and the whole were not of *yours,* but of *Nature's* making. The metaphor is taken from a piece of mechanism finished by some great master, where all the parts are so previously fitted, as to be easily put together by any ordinary workman: and each part slides into its place, as it were thro' a groove ready made for that purpose.[64]

It is this air of inevitability, of wholeness, of "rightness," with its attendant satisfactions for the beholder, that an intelligent manipulation of the parts can bring about; but it must always be primarily the whole, never the parts in and for themselves, which is foremost in the designer's mind. Therefore, when ornamental detail is worshipped for its own sake alone, whether in painting or poetry or architecture or landscaping, its influence has at that moment become unnatural and distracting.

In the celebrated passage describing Timon's villa and its surroundings (lines 99-168) Pope paints a horrible picture of what he understands by the lack of taste and sense and by the absence of any ability or inclination to follow Nature. At Timon's villa, "Where all cry out, 'What sums are thrown away!'" conspicuous consumption has reached the final extremity of nonsense. Everything is enormous and expensive, and amid these "huge heaps of littleness" (line 109) stands Timon himself, "A puny insect, shiv'ring at a breeze!" ludicrously dwarfed by the Brobdingnagian immensity of all that his vulgar tastes have created. After the delight-

---

63 For a much earlier statement on order, harmony, and wholeness in landscaping, cf. *Windsor Forest* (1713), lines 11-20.

64 Warburton, 275. The italics are Warburton's.

ful impudence of the squirting Cupids (line 111), Pope calls particular attention to Timon's gardens, as tasteless and as tiresome in their extreme regularity as the prodigious villa itself. Like Addison in *Spectator* No. 412, Pope prizes an artful variety; indeed, he has already remarked earlier in the epistle,

> He gains all points, who pleasingly confounds,
> Surprizes, varies, and conceals the Bounds.
> (Lines 55-56)

But at Timon's gardens there is no such variety:

> No pleasing Intricacies intervene,
> No artful wildness to perplex the scene;
> Grove nods at grove, each Alley has a brother,
> And half the platform just reflects the other.
> (Lines 115-118)

In all this tedious symmetry there is no trace of what Pope had years before described as the "nameless graces which no methods teach," no trace of the inexplicable and inspired beauties which deviate boldly from the regularity of rule and lie "beyond the reach of art" (*Essay on Criticism*, lines 141-158). The tame smoothness of Pope's poetry in lines 117-118—he is a master of onomatopoeia—captures all this dullness to perfection. But humdrum regularity is by no means the worst of it. In obedience to a common contemporary fad, Timon has had his bushes tonsured into the shapes of animals and people (lines 119-126), an outrageous disfigurement of Nature which Pope had ridiculed as far back as No. 173 of *The Guardian*. The relationship between the geometrical arrangement of formal gardens and the habit of clipping shrubbery into unnatural shapes is brought out by Addison in *Spectator* No. 414, where he discusses them together:

> Our British gardeners . . . instead of humouring nature, love to deviate from it as much as possible.

> Our trees rise in cones, globes, and pyramids.
> [Timon's, of course, are in gladiators and seahorses.]
> We see the marks of the scissors upon every plant
> and bush. I do not know whether I am singular in
> my opinion, but, for my own part, I would rather
> look upon a tree in all its luxuriancy and diffusion of
> boughs and branches, than when it is thus cut and
> trimmed into a mathematical figure; and cannot but
> fancy that an orchard in flower looks infinitely more
> delightful than all the little labyrinths of the most
> finished parterre.

This is approximately Pope's position. As Timon's architectural tastes are unnaturally heavy, his taste in gardening is unnaturally effete; in either case the end result is a ludicrous violation of the Horatian canons of simplicity and naturalness which Pope had enunciated as early as the *Essay on Criticism*. Pope wickedly emphasizes the foolish anomalies brought about by these sculptured bushes ("Un-water'd see the drooping sea-horse mourn," line 125), just as he had done two decades earlier with a droll little catalogue of such nonsense in *The Guardian*: "Noah's ark in Holly, the ribs a little damaged for want of water . . . A topping Ben Jonson in Laurel . . . A quick-set Hog shot up into a Porcupine by being forgot a week in rainy weather . . ." and so on.

The visitor is then vouchsafed a brief glimpse of Timon's study, where the most imposing volumes, like those in Leonora's library, are of wood; followed by a moment devoted to "the Pride of Pray'r" (line 142) beneath the fleshly baroque painted ceiling of Timon's chapel, where the "soft Dean" invites the faithful to slumber and "never mentions Hell to ears polite" (line 150). After these suitably perfunctory acknowledgments of serious matters, Timon's guests are summoned in to dinner. This is the crowning triumph of vulgarity. So far we have seen only that Timon does not know how to decorate a house or arrange a garden. This is bad enough, but it now becomes clear that he does not even know how to live. Perhaps this ultimate ignorance should come as no surprise, in the light of what we have already been told, but the discomforts of the meal that follows are beyond belief. Now the ostentatious pride of Timon's house and the rigid formalism of Timon's gardens overwhelmingly combine to destroy any possibility of gracious and leisurely dining. The pompous ceremony of the service, with its overtones of Roman sacrifice and Christian liturgy, makes everyone ill at ease; and the furious haste with which course follows course makes it impossible for the guests even to be helped to what they want, let alone to enjoy their food. All sense of hospitality and gracious entertainment is submerged in what amounts to the Ruling Passion of Timon's life, the desire to display his wealth. Thus his tastelessness and his vanity in his own possessions not only ruin the appearance of his expensive dwelling; what is worse, they ruin the meal and with it all hope of decent human relationships of any kind. The guests go home with curses in their hearts (lines 165-168), and Timon is left where we found him, standing amid his costly piles of littleness, dwarfed, ridiculous, and alone. Like the unhappy Duke of Wharton in the *Epistle to Cobham*, his is "A constant Bounty which no friend has made," a bounty which pleases no one because it is born of neither taste nor generosity nor friendship nor a desire to be of use, but only of a fanatic eagerness to impress.

And yet, Pope adds, there is a paradoxical and even a providential sense in which Timon's extravagance is useful just the same, for conspicuous consumption and conspicuous waste have the effect of consuming goods on a lavish scale; thus, indirectly, they provide employment. Pope expresses the idea in a neat paradox:

> What his hard Heart denies,
His charitable Vanity supplies.

(Lines 171-172)

This is a characteristic attitude in Pope. A major theme of
the *Essay on Man* is God's way of bringing real good out of
apparent evil—and before we are tempted to construe this
belief as mere shallow optimism, we need to recall its similarity to a basic fact of Christian theology, that out of the
apparent evil of the Fall of Man came the Incarnation and
the Resurrection. Good may emerge in this way even out
of the madness of Atossa in the *Epistle to a Lady*, for she is
childless and has no heir. Consequently,

> To Heirs unknown descends th' unguarded store,
> Or wanders, Heav'n-directed, to the Poor.
>
> (*Epistle to a Lady*, lines 149-150)

Warburton's note to these lines speaks of "the great principle
of [Pope's] Philosophy, which he never loses sight of, and
which teaches, that Providence is incessantly turning the
evils arising from the follies and the vices of men to general
good."[65] And this is a principle which we have already seen
at work in the *Epistle to Bathurst*, where we are told that

> "Extremes in Nature equal good produce,
> "Extremes in Man concur to gen'ral use."
>
> (*Epistle to Bathurst*, lines 163-164)

Despite these comforting reflections, however, it will not
be very long before all of Timon's monstrous extravagance
will have disappeared, to be supplanted by something whose
beauty is simple and natural and whose usefulness is more
than merely indirect:

> Another age shall see the golden Ear
> Imbrown the Slope, and nod on the Parterre,
> Deep Harvests bury all his pride has plann'd,
> And laughing Ceres re-assume the land.
>
> (*Epistle to Burlington*, lines 173-176)

---

65 Warburton, 203.

Here Pope is saying pretty much what Addison says in the last sentence of the passage from *Spectator* No. 414 given above. But Pope is saying more. He has couched in one of his characteristically Roman utterances the Roman virtues of simplicity and usefulness which form the thematic basis of the poem. This is no such cornfield as an English peasant would have recognized, heavy with heat and dust, clouded with insects and redolent of manure. It is just such a cornfield as could only be personified in "laughing Ceres," a beautifully georgic and melodious phrase which conjures up visions of Horace and Vergil, of Roman statuary and the Corycian swain—a phrase which marks Pope's own vision as that of an ideal cornfield far removed from the grimy scene of a laborer's toil or even from a canvas by Constable. (The phrase "laughing Ceres," like Marvell's "Deserts of vast eternity," loses most of its music when pronounced in the American way: "laffing Ceres." Pope's own pronunciation must have been a good deal less nasal, something like "lahfing Serraze.") But "laughing Ceres" is more than a marble statue or a mere neo-classic cliché; it is a symbol and almost a Platonic ideal. It symbolizes the triumph of that which is valuable in itself over that which is valuable only because it is expensive. It symbolizes the inevitable downfall of fruitless artificiality and gaudy and unprofitable show, the inevitable victory of Roman practicality, simplicity, and common sense. (And this is a victory, be it noted, which is just as necessary in poetry as it is in architecture and gardening.) Rather than any literal reality of fields and harvests, what Pope is getting at in these four lines is a universal truth, as he thinks it—that pointless and self-gratifying profusion must sooner or later give way to something of genuine worth. This he has already explained in the *Epistle to Bathurst* (lines 171-178). And using the idea as a transitional point, Pope now moves on to conclude his poem on an affirmative note. Emphasizing this very point of direct, as against involuntary, usefulness, Pope says in substance that men like Burlington (called Boyle in line 178), who spend their money not on meaningless ostentation but on works which profit their fellow countrymen and enrich their native land—that such men are those who are really raising monuments for the ages:

> These Honours, Peace, to happy Britain brings,
> These are Imperial Works, and worthy Kings.

The Man of Ross is only metaphorically related to Caesar Augustus (*Epistle to Bathurst,* lines 249-258); the public philanthropies of the Earl of Burlington make him an emperor in his own right.

EPISTLES TO SEVERAL PERSONS

(Moral Essays)

Est brevitate opus, ut currat sententia, neu se
Impediat verbis lassas onerantibus aures:
Et sermone opus est modo tristi, sæpe jocoso,
Defendente vicem modo Rhetoris atque Poetæ,
Interdum urbani, parcentis viribus, atque
Extenuantis eas consultò.—Hor. [Satires i. x. 9-14]

[Close be your language; let your sense be clear,
Nor with a weight of words fatigue the ear;
From grave to jovial you must change with art,
Now play the critic's, now the poet's part;
In raillery assume a graver air,
Discreetly hide your strength, your vigor spare;
For ridicule shall frequently prevail,
And cut the knot when graver reasons fail.

—Sir Philip Francis]

EPISTLE I

TO

Sir *Richard Temple,* Lord *Cobham*

ARGUMENT[1]

Of the Knowledge *and* Characters *of* MEN

THAT it is not sufficient for this knowledge to consider Man in the Abstract: Books *will not serve the purpose, nor yet our own* Experience *singly,* v. 1. *General maxims, unless they be formed upon* both, *will be but notional,* v. 10. *Some Peculiarity in every man, characteristic to himself, yet varying from himself,* v. 15. *Difficulties arising from our own Passions, Fancies, Faculties,* &c. v. 31 [23]. *The shortness of Life, to observe in, and the uncertainty of the* Principles of action *in men to observe by,* v. 37 [29], &c. *Our own Principle of action often hid from ourselves,* v. 41. *No judging of the* Motives *from the actions; the same actions proceeding from contrary Motives, and the same Motives influencing contrary actions,* v. 100 [51]. *Yet to form* Characters, *we can only take the* strongest actions *of a man's life, and try to make them* agree: *The utter uncertainty of this, from* Nature *itself, and from* Policy, v. 120 [71]. Characters *given according to the* rank *of men of the world,* v. 135 [87]. *And some reason for it,* v. 140 [93]. Education *alters the* Nature, *or at least* Character *of many,* v. 149 [101]. *Some few Characters plain, but in general confounded, dissembled, or inconsistent,* v. 51 [122]. *The same man utterly different in different places and seasons,* v. 71 [130]. *Unimaginable weaknesses in the greatest,* v. 70 [140], &c. *Nothing constant and certain but* God *and* Nature, v. 95 [154]. Actions, Passions, Opinions, Manners, Humours, *or* Principles *all subject to change. No judging by* Nature, *from* v. 158 to 178 [173]. *It only remains to find (if we can) his* Ruling Passion

91

That will certainly influence all the rest, and can reconcile the seeming or real inconsistency of all his actions, v. 175 [174]. *Instanced in the extraordinary character of* [Wharton], v. 179. *A caution against mistaking* second qualities *for* first, *which will destroy all possibility of the knowledge of mankind,* v. 210. *Examples of the strength of the* Ruling Passion, *and its continuation to the last breath,* v. 222, &c.

EPISTLE I

To Sir Richard Temple, Lord Cobham²

Yes, you despise the man to Books confin'd,
Who from his study rails at human kind;
Tho' what he learns he speaks, and may advance
Some gen'ral maxims, or be right by chance.
The coxcomb bird, so talkative and grave,   5
That from his cage cries Cuckold, Whore, and Knave,
Tho' many a passenger³ he rightly call,
You hold him no Philosopher at all.
    And yet the fate of all extremes is such,
Men may be read, as well as Books, too much.   10
To observations which ourselves we make,
We grow more partial for th' Observer's sake;
To written Wisdom, as another's, less:
Maxims are drawn from Notions, those from Guess.⁴
There's some Peculiar in each leaf and grain,   15
Some unmark'd fibre, or some varying vein:
Shall only Man be taken in the gross?
Grant but as many sorts of Mind as Moss.
    That each from other differs, first confess;
Next, that he varies from himself no less: 20
Add Nature's, Custom's, Reason's, Passion's strife,
And all Opinion's colours cast on life.
    Yet more; the diff'rence is as great between
The optics seeing, as the objects seen.
All Manners take a tincture from our own;   25
Or come discolour'd thro' our Passions shown.
Or Fancy's beam enlarges, multiplies,
Contracts, inverts, and gives ten thousand dyes.
    Our depths who fathoms, or our shallows finds,
Quick whirls, and shifting eddies, of our minds?   30
Life's stream for Observation will not stay,⁵
It hurries all too fast to mark their way:

In vain sedate reflections we wou'd make,
When half our knowledge we must snatch, not take.[6]
On human actions reason tho' you can,   35
It may be Reason, but it is not Man:[7]
His Principle of action once explore,
That instant 'tis his Principle no more.
Like following life thro' creatures you dissect,
You lose it in the moment you detect.   40

   Oft, in the Passions' wild rotation tost,
Our spring of action to ourselves is lost:
Tir'd, not determin'd, to the last we yield,
And what comes then is master of the field.
As the last image of that troubled heap,   45
When Sense subsides, and Fancy sports in sleep,
(Tho' past the recollection of the thought)
Becomes the stuff of which our dream is wrought:
Something as dim to our internal view,
Is thus, perhaps, the cause of most we do.   50

   In vain the Sage, with retrospective eye,
Would from th' apparent What conclude the Why,
Infer the Motive from the Deed, and shew,
That what we chanc'd was what we meant to do.
Behold! If Fortune or a Mistress frowns,   55
Some plunge in bus'ness, others shave their crowns:
To ease the Soul of one oppressive weight,
This quits an Empire, that embroils a State:
The same adust[8] complexion has impell'd
Charles to the Convent, Philip to the Field.[9]   60

   Not always Actions shew the man: we find
Who does a kindness, is not therefore kind;
Perhaps Prosperity becalm'd his breast,
Perhaps the Wind just shifted from the east:
Not therefore humble he who seeks retreat,   65
Pride guides his steps, and bids him shun the great:
Who combats bravely is not therefore brave,

He dreads a death-bed like the meanest slave:
Who reasons wisely is not therefore wise,
His pride in Reas'ning, not in Acting lies.[10]   70
    But grant that Actions best discover man;
Take the most strong, and sort them as you can.
The few that glare each character must mark,
You balance not the many in the dark.
What will you do with such as disagree?   75
Suppress them, or miscall them Policy?[11]
Must then at once (the character to save)
The plain rough Hero turn a crafty Knave?
Alas! in truth the man but chang'd his mind,
Perhaps was sick, in love, or had not din'd.   80
Ask why from Britain Cæsar would retreat?
Cæsar himself might whisper he was beat.
Why risk the world's great empire for a Punk?
Cæsar perhaps might answer he was drunk.[12]
But, sage historians! 'tis your task to prove   85
One action Conduct; one, heroic Love.
    'Tis from high Life high Characters are drawn;
A Saint in Crape is twice a Saint in Lawn;[13]
A Judge is just, a Chanc'lor juster still;
A Gownman, learn'd; a Bishop, what you will;   90
Wise, if a Minister; but, if a King,
More wise, more learn'd, more just, more ev'rything.[14]
Court-virtues bear, like Gems, the highest rate,
Born where Heav'n's influence scarce can penetrate:
In life's low vale, the soil the virtues like,   95
They please as beauties, here as wonders strike.
Tho' the same Sun with all-diffusive rays
Blush in the Rose, and in the Di'mond blaze,
We prize the stronger effort of his pow'r,
And justly set the Gem above the Flow'r.[15]   100
    'Tis Education forms the common mind,
Just as the Twig is bent, the Tree's inclin'd.

Boastful and rough, your first son is a 'Squire;
The next a Tradesman, meek, and much a lyar;
Tom struts a Soldier, open, bold, and brave;   105
Will sneaks a Scriv'ner, an exceeding knave:

Is he a Churchman? then he's fond of pow'r: ⎫
A Quaker? sly: a Presbyterian? sow'r: ⎬
A smart Free-thinker? all things in an hour. ⎭

True, some are open, and to all men known;   110
Others so very close, they're hid from none;
(So Darkness strike the sense no less than Light)
Thus gracious CHANDOS[16] is belov'd at sight;
And ev'ry child hates Shylock,[17] tho' his soul
Still sits at squat, and peeps not from its hole.   115

At half mankind when gen'rous Manly[18] raves,
All know 'tis Virtue, for he thinks them knaves:
When universal homage Umbra[19] pays,
All see 'tis Vice, and itch of vulgar praise.
When Flatt'ry glares, all hate it in a Queen,[20]   120
While one there is who charms us with his Spleen.[21]

But these plain Characters we rarely find;
Tho' strong the bent, yet quick the turns of mind:
Or puzzling Contraries confound the whole;
Or Affectations quite reverse the soul.   125
The Dull, flat Falshood serves, for policy:
And in the Cunning, Truth itself's a lye:[22]
Unthought-of Frailties cheat us in the Wise;
The Fool lies hid in inconsistencies.[23]

See the same man, in vigour, in the gout;   130
Alone, in company; in place, or out:
Early at Bus'ness, and at Hazard late;
Mad at a Fox-chace, wise at a Debate;
Drunk at a Borough, civil at a Ball;
Friendly at Hackney,[24] faithless at Whitehall.[25]   135

Catius[26] is ever moral, ever grave,

Thinks who endures a knave, is next a knave,
Save just at dinner—then prefers, no doubt,
A Rogue with Ven'son to a Saint without.
    Who would not praise Patritio's[27] high desert,   140
His hand unstain'd, his uncorrupted heart,
His comprehensive head! all Int'rests weigh'd,
All Europe sav'd, yet Britain not betray'd.
He thanks you not, his pride is in Picquette,[28]
New-market-fame,[29] and judgment at a Bett.   145
    [Triumphant Leaders, at an Army's head,
Hemm'd round with Glories, pilfer cloth or bread,
As meanly plunder, as they bravely fought,
Now save a People, and now save a groat.][30]
    What made (say Montagne, or more sage Charron!)[31] 146
Otho[32] a warrior, Cromwell[33] a buffoon?
A perjur'd Prince a leaden Saint revere,[34]
A godless Regent tremble at a Star?[35]
The throne a Bigot keep, a Genius quit,   150
Faithless thro' Piety, and dup'd thro' Wit?[36]
Europe a Woman, Child, or Dotard rule,
And just her wisest monarch made a fool?[37]
    Know GOD and NATURE only are the same:
In Man, the judgment shoots at flying game,   155
A bird of passage! gone as soon as found,
Now in the Moon perhaps, now under ground.[38]
    Ask men's Opinions: Scoto[39] now shall tell
How Trade increases, and the World goes well;
Strike off his Pension, by the setting sun,   160
And Britain, if not Europe, is undone.
    That gay Free-thinker, a fine talker once,
What turns him now a stupid silent dunce?
Some God, or Spirit he has lately found;
Or chanc'd to meet a Minister that frown'd.[40]   165
    Manners with Fortunes, Humours turn with Climes,
Tenets with Books, and Principles with Times.[41]

Judge we by Nature? Habit can efface,
Int'rest o'ercome, or Policy take place:
By Actions? those Uncertainty divides: 170
By Passions? these Dissimulation hides:
Opinions? they still take a wider range:
Find, if you can, in what you cannot change.
   Search then the Ruling Passion:[42] There, alone,
The Wild are constant, and the Cunning known;   175
The Fool consistent, and the False sincere;
Priests, Princes, Women,[43] no dissemblers here.
This clue once found, unravels all the rest,
The prospect clears, and Wharton[44] stands confest.
Wharton, the scorn and wonder of our days,   180
Whose ruling Passion was the Lust of Praise:
Born with whate'er could win it from the Wise,
Women and Fools must like him or he dies;
Tho' wond'ring Senates hung on all he spoke,
The Club [45] must hail him master of the joke.   185
Shall parts so various aim at nothing new?
He'll shine a Tully and a Wilmot[46] too.
Then turns repentant, and his God adores
With the same spirit that he drinks and whores;
Enough if all around him but admire,   190
And now the Punk applaud, and now the Fryer.
Thus with each gift of nature and of art,
And wanting nothing but an honest heart;
Grown all to all, from no one vice exempt;
And most contemptible, to shun contempt;   195
His Passion still, to covet gen'ral praise,
His Life, to forfeit it a thousand ways;
A constant Bounty which no friend has made;
An angel Tongue, which no man can persuade;
A Fool, with more of Wit than half mankind,   200
Too rash for thought, for Action too refin'd:
A Tyrant to the wife his heart approves;[47]

A Rebel to the very king he loves;
He dies, sad out-cast of each church and state,
And, harder still! flagitious, yet not great.   205
Ask you why Wharton broke thro' ev'ry rule?
'Twas all for fear the Knaves should call him Fool.

    Nature well known, no prodigies remain,
Comets are regular, and Wharton plain.

    Yet, in this search, the wisest may mistake,   210
If second qualities for first they take.
When Catiline[48] by rapine swell'd his store;
When Cæsar made a noble dame a whore;[49]
In this the Lust, in that the Avarice
Were means, not ends; Ambition was the vice.   215
That very Cæsar, born in Scipio's[50] days,
Had aim'd, like him, by Chastity at praise.
Lucullus,[51] when Frugality could charm,
Had roasted turnips in the Sabin farm.
In vain th' observer eyes the builder's toil,   220
But quite mistakes the scaffold for the pile.

    In this one Passion man can strength enjoy,
As Fits give vigour, just when they destroy.
Time, that on all things lays his lenient hand,
Yet tames not this;[52] it sticks to our last sand.   225
Consistent in our follies and our sins,
Here honest Nature ends as she begins.

    Behold a rev'rend sire, whom want of grace
Has made the father of a nameless race,
Shov'd from the wall perhaps, or rudely press'd   230
By his own son, that passes by unbless'd:
Still to his wench he crawls on knocking knees,
And envies ev'ry sparrow that he sees.[53]

    A salmon's belly, Helluo, was thy fate;
The doctor call'd, declares all help too late: 235
"Mercy! cries Helluo, mercy on my soul!
"Is there no hope?—Alas!—then bring the jowl."[54]

The frugal Crone, whom praying priests attend,
Still tries to save the hallow'd taper's end,
Collects her breath, as ebbing life retires,   240
For one puff more, and in that puff expires.[55]

"Odious! in woollen! 'twould a Saint provoke,
(Were the last words that poor Narcissa spoke)
"No, let a charming Chintz, and Brussels lace
"Wrap my cold limbs, and shade my lifeless face: 245
"One would not, sure, be frightful when one's dead—
"And—Betty—give this Cheek a little Red."[56]

Old Politicians chew on wisdom past,
And totter on in bus'ness to the last;
As weak, as earnest; and as gravely out,   250
As sober Lanesb'row[57] dancing in the gout.

The Courtier smooth, who forty years had shin'd
An humble servant to all human kind,
Just brought out this, when scarce his tongue could stir,
"If—where I'm going—I could serve you, Sir?"   255

"I give and I devise (old Euclio[58] said,
And sigh'd) "my lands and tenements to Ned."
Your money, Sir; "My money, Sir, what all?
"Why,—if I must—(then wept) I give it Paul."
The Manor, Sir?—"The Manor! hold, he cry'd,   260
"Not that,—I cannot part with that"—and dy'd.
And you! brave COBHAM, to the latest breath
Shall feel your ruling passion strong in death:
Such in those moments as in all the past,
"Oh, save my country, Heav'n!" shall be your last.[59]   265

EPISTLE II

To a LADY

Of the CHARACTERS *of* WOMEN

ARGUMENT[1]

Of the Characters of *Women* (consider'd only as contra-distinguished from the other Sex.) That these are yet more inconsistent and incomprehensible than those of Men, of which Instances are given even from such Characters as are plainest, and most strongly mark'd; as in the *Affected,* VER. 7, &c. The *Soft-natur'd,* 29. the *Cunning,* 45. the *Whimsical,* 50 [53]. the *Wits* and *Refiners,* 69 [87]. the *Stupid* and *Silly,* 80 [101]. How Contrarieties run thro' them all.

But tho' the *Particular Characters* of this Sex are more various than those of Men, the *General Characteristick,* as to the *Ruling Passion,* is more uniform and confin'd. In what That lies, and whence it proceeds, 109 [207], &c. Men are best known in publick Life, Women in private, 110 [199]. What are the *Aims,* and the *Fate* of the Sex, both as to *Power* and *Pleasure?* 121, 133 [219, 231], &c. Advice for their true Interest, 151 [249]. The Picture of an esteemable Woman, made up of the best Kind of Contrarieties, 171 [296], &c.

CARL A. RUDISILL LIBRARY
LENOIR RHYNE COLLEGE

EPISTLE II

TO

A LADY[2]

Of the Characters of Women

Nothing so true as what you once let fall,
"Most Women have no Characters at all."
Matter too soft a lasting mark to bear,
And best distinguish'd by black, brown, or fair.
    How many pictures of one Nymph we view,[3]   5
All how unlike each other, all how true!
Arcadia's Countess,[4] here, in ermin'd pride,
Is there, Pastora by a fountain side.
Here Fannia,[5] leering on her own good man,
And there, a naked Leda with a Swan.   10
Let then the Fair one beautifully cry,
In Magdalen's loose hair and lifted eye,
Or drest in smiles of sweet Cecilia[6] shine,
With simp'ring Angels, Palms, and Harps divine;
Whether the Charmer sinner it, or saint it,   15
If Folly grow romantic,[7] I must paint it.
    Come then, the colours and the ground prepare!
Dip in the Rainbow, trick her off in Air;
Chuse a firm Cloud, before it fall, and in it
Catch, e'er she change, the Cynthia of this minute.   20
    Rufa, whose eye quick-glancing o'er the Park,[8]
Attracts each light gay meteor of a Spark,
Agrees as ill with Rufa studying Locke,[9]
As Sappho's[10] di'monds with her dirty smock;
Or Sappho at her toilet's greasy task,   25
With Sappho fragrant at an ev'ning Mask:
So morning Insects that in muck begun,
Shine, buzz, and fly-blow in the setting-sun.

How soft is Silia! fearful to offend;[11]
The Frail one's advocate, the Weak one's friend: 30
To her, Calista prov'd her conduct nice;
And good Simplicius asks of her advice.
Sudden, she storms! she raves! You tip the wink,
But spare your censure; Silia does not drink.
All eyes may see from what the change arose,   35
All eyes may see—a Pimple on her nose.[12]
    Papillia, wedded to her am'rous spark,
Sighs for the shades—"How charming is a Park!"
A Park is purchas'd, but the Fair he sees
All bath'd in tears—"Oh odious, odious Trees!"[13]   40
    Ladies, like variegated Tulips, show;
'Tis to their Changes half their charms we owe;
Fine by defect, and delicately weak,
Their happy Spots the nice admirer take,
'Twas thus Calypso once each heart alarm'd,[14]   45
Aw'd without Virtue, without Beauty charm'd;
Her Tongue bewitch'd as odly as her Eyes,
Less Wit than Mimic, more a Wit than wise;
Strange graces still, and stranger flights she had,
Was just not ugly, and was just not mad;   50
Yet ne'er so sure our passion to create,
As when she touch'd the brink of all we hate.[15]
    Narcissa's nature, tolerably mild,[16]
To make a wash, would hardly stew a child;
Has ev'n been prov'd to grant a Lover's pray'r,   55
And paid a Tradesman once to make him stare;
Gave alms at Easter, in a Christian trim,
And made a Widow happy, for a whim.
Why then declare Good-nature is her scorn,
When 'tis by that alone she can be born?   60
Why pique all mortals, yet affect a name?
A fool to Pleasure, yet a slave to Fame:
Now deep in Taylor[17] and the Book of Martyrs,[18]

Now drinking citron[19] with his Grace[20] and Chartres:[21]
Now Conscience chills her, and now Passion burns;   65
And Atheism and Religion take their turns;
A very Heathen in the carnal part.
Yet still a sad, good Christian at her heart.[22]
   See Sin in State, majestically drunk;[23]
Proud as a Peeress, prouder as a Punk;   70
Chaste to her Husband, frank to all beside,
A teeming Mistress, but a barren Bride.
What then? let Blood and Body bear the fault,
Her Head's untouch'd, that noble Seat of Thought:
Such this day's doctrine—in another fit   75
She sins with Poets thro' pure Love of Wit.
What has not fir'd her bosom or her brain?
Cæsar and Tall-boy, Charles and Charlema'ne.[24]
As Helluo,[25] late Dictator of the Feast,
The Nose of Hautgout, and the Tip of Taste,   80
Critick'd your wine, and analyz'd your meat,
Yet on plain Pudding deign'd at-home to eat;
So Philomedé, lect'ring all mankind
On the soft Passion, and the Taste refin'd,
Th' Address, the Delicacy—stoops at once,   85
And makes her hearty meal upon a Dunce.[26]
   Flavia's a Wit, has too much sense to Pray;[27]
To Toast our wants and wishes, is her way;
Nor asks of God, but of her Stars, to give
The mighty blessing, "while we live, to live."   90
Then all for Death, that Opiate of the soul!
Lucretia's dagger, Rosamonda's bowl.[28]
Say, what can cause such impotence of mind?
A Spark too fickle, or a Spouse too kind.
Wise Wretch! with Pleasures too refin'd to please;   95
With too much Spirit to be e'er at ease;
With too much Quickness ever to be taught;
With too much Thinking to have common Thought:

You purchase Pain with all that Joy can give,
And die of nothing but a Rage to live.   100
    Turn then from Wits; and look on Simo's Mate,[29]
No Ass so meek, no Ass so obstinate.
Or her, that owns her Faults, but never mends,
Because she's honest, and the best of Friends.
Or her, whose life the Church and Scandal share,   105
For ever in a Passion, or a Pray'r.[30]
Or her, who laughs at Hell, but (like her Grace)[31]
Cries, "Ah! how charming, if there's no such place!"
Or who in sweet vicissitude appears
Of Mirth and Opium, Ratafie[32] and Tears,   110
The daily Anodyne, and nightly Draught,
To kill those foes to Fair ones, Time and Thought.
Woman and Fool are two hard things to hit;
For true No-meaning puzzles more than Wit.
    But what are these to great Atossa's mind?[33]   115
Scarce once herself, by turns all Womankind!
Who, with herself, or others, from her birth
Finds all her life one warfare upon earth:
Shines, in exposing Knaves, and painting Fools,
Yet is, whate'er she hates and ridicules.   120
No Thought advances, but her Eddy Brain
Whisks it about, and down it goes again.[34]
Full sixty years the World has been her Trade,
The wisest Fool much Time has ever made.
From loveless youth to unrespected age,   125
No Passion gratify'd except her Rage.
So much the Fury still out-ran the Wit,
The Pleasure miss'd her, and the Scandal hit.
Who breaks with her, provokes Revenge from Hell,
But he's a bolder man who dares be well.   130
Her ev'ry turn with Violence pursu'd,
Nor more a storm her Hate than Gratitude:
To that each Passion turns, or soon or late;

Love, if it makes her yield, must make her hate:
Superiors? death! and Equals? what a curse!   135
But an Inferior not dependant? worse.
Offend her, and she knows not to forgive;
Oblige her, and she'll hate you while you live:
But die, and she'll adore you—Then the Bust
And Temple rise—then fall again to dust.   140
Last night, her Lord was all that's good and great;
A Knave this morning, and his Will a Cheat.
Strange! by the Means defeated of the Ends,
By Spirit robb'd of Pow'r, by Warmth of Friends,
By Wealth of Follow'rs! without one distress   145
Sick of herself thro' very selfishness!
Atossa, curs'd with ev'ry granted pray'r,
Childless with all her Children, wants an Heir.[35]
To Heirs unknown descends th'unguarded store,
Or wanders, Heav'n-directed, to the Poor.[36]   150
  Pictures like these, dear Madam, to design,
Asks no firm hand, and no unerring line;
Some wand'ring touches, some reflected light,
Some flying stroke alone can hit 'em right:[37]
For how should equal Colours do the knack?   155
Chameleons who can paint in white and black?
  "Yet Cloe[38] sure was form'd without a spot"—
Nature in her then err'd not, but forgot.
"With ev'ry pleasing, ev'ry prudent part,
"Say, what can Cloe want?"—She wants a Heart.   160
She speaks, behaves, and acts just as she ought;
But never, never, reach'd one gen'rous Thought.
Virtue she finds too painful an endeavour,
Content to dwell in Decencies for ever.
So very reasonable, so unmov'd,   165
As never yet to love, or to be lov'd.
She, while her Lover pants upon her breast,
Can mark the figures on an Indian chest;

And when she sees her Friend in deep despair,
Observes how much a Chintz exceeds Mohair.   170
Forbid it Heav'n, a Favour or a Debt
She e'er should cancel—but she may forget.
Safe is your Secret still in Cloe's ear;
But none of Cloe's shall you ever hear.
Of all her Dears she never slander'd one,   175
But cares not if a thousand are undone.
Would Cloe know if you're alive or dead?
She bids her Footman put it in her head.[39]
Cloe is prudent—Would you too be wise?
Then never break your heart when Cloe dies.   180
    One certain Portrait may (I grant) be seen,
Which Heav'n has varnish'd out, and made a *Queen*:[40]
THE SAME FOR EVER! and describ'd by all
With Truth and Goodness, as with Crown and Ball.
Poets heap Virtues, Painters Gems at will,   185
And show their zeal, and hide their want of skill.[41]
'Tis well—but, Artists! who can paint or write,
To draw the Naked is your true delight.
That Robe of Quality so struts and swells,
None see what Parts of Nature it conceals:[42]   190
Th'exactest traits of Body or of Mind,
We owe to models of an humble kind.
If QUEENSBERRY[43] to strip there's no compelling,
'Tis from a Handmaid we must take a Helen.
From Peer or Bishop 'tis no easy thing   195
To draw the man who loves his God, or King:
Alas! I copy (or my draught would fail)
From honest Mah'met, or plain Parson Hale.[44]
    But grant, in Public Men sometimes are shown, [45]
A Woman's seen in Private life alone: 200
Our bolder Talents in full light display'd;
Your Virtues open fairest in the shade.
Bred to disguise,[46] in Public 'tis you hide;

There, none distinguish 'twixt your Shame or Pride,
Weakness or Delicacy; all so nice,   205
That each may seem a Virtue, or a Vice.[47]
   In Men, we various Ruling Passions find; [48]
In Women, two almost divide the kind;
Those, only fix'd, they first or last obey,
The Love of Pleasure, and the Love of Sway.   210
   That,[49] Nature gives; and where the lesson taught[50]
Is but to please, can Pleasure seem a fault?
Experience, this;[51] by Man's oppression curst,
They seek the second not to lose the first.
   Men, some to Bus'ness, some to Pleasure take;   215
But ev'ry Woman is at heart a Rake:[52]
Men, some to Quiet, some to public Strife;
But ev'ry Lady would be Queen for life.
   Yet mark the fate of a whole Sex of Queens![53]
Pow'r all their end, but Beauty all the means: 220
In Youth they conquer, with so wild a rage,
As leaves them scarce a subject in their Age:
For foreign glory, foreign joy, they roam;
No thought of peace or happiness at home.
But Wisdom's triumph is well-tim'd Retreat,   225
As hard a science to the Fair as Great!
Beauties, like Tyrants, old and friendless grown,
Yet hate repose, and dread to be alone,
Worn out in public, weary ev'ry eye,
Nor leave one sigh behind them when they die.   230
   Pleasures the sex, as children Birds, pursue,[54]
Still out of reach, yet never out of view;
Sure, if they catch, to spoil the Toy at most,
To covet flying, and regret when lost:
At last, to follies Youth could scarce defend,   235
It grows their Age's prudence to pretend;
Asham'd to own they gave delight before,
Reduc'd to feign it, when they give no more:

As Hags hold Sabbaths, less for joy than spight,
So these their merry, miserable Night;   240
Still round and round the Ghosts of Beauty glide,
And haunt the places where their Honour dy'd.[55]
    See how the World its Veterans rewards!
A Youth of Frolicks, an old Age of Cards;
Fair to no purpose, artful to no end,   245
Young without Lovers, old without a Friend;
A Fop their Passion, but their Prize a Sot,
Alive, ridiculous, and dead, forgot![56]
    Ah! Friend! to dazzle let the Vain design;[57]
To raise the Thought, and touch the Heart be thine!   250
That Charm shall grow, while what fatigues the Ring,[58]
Flaunts and goes down, an unregarded thing:
So when the Sun's broad beam has tir'd the sight,
All mild ascends the Moon's more sober light,
Serene in Virgin Modesty she shines,   255
And unobserv'd the glaring Orb declines.[59]
    Oh! blest with Temper, whose unclouded ray
Can make to-morrow chearful as to-day;
She, who can love a Sister's charms, or hear
Sighs for a Daughter with unwounded ear;   260
She, who ne'er answers till a Husband cools,
Or, if she rules him, never shows she rules;
Charms by accepting, by submitting sways,
Yet has her humour most, when she obeys:
Let Fops or Fortune fly which way they will;   265
Disdains all loss of Tickets, or Codille;[60]
Spleen, Vapours, or Small-pox,[61] above them all,
And Mistress of herself, tho' China fall.[62]
    And yet, believe me, good as well as ill,[63]
Woman's at best a Contradiction still.   270
Heav'n, when it strives to polish all it can
Its last best work, but forms a softer Man;
Picks from each sex, to make the Fav'rite blest,

Your love of Pleasure, our desire of Rest:
Blends, in exception to all gen'ral rules,   275
Your Taste of Follies, with our Scorn of Fools:
Reserve with Frankness, Art with Truth ally'd,
Courage with softness, Modesty with Pride;
Fix'd Principles, with Fancy ever new;
Shakes all together, and produces—You.   280
   Be this a Woman's Fame: with this unblest,
Toasts live a scorn, and Queens may die a jest.
This Phoebus promis'd (I forget the year)[64]
When those blue eyes first open'd on the sphere;
Ascendant Phoebus watch'd that hour with care,[65]   285
Averted half your Parents' simple Pray'r;
And gave you Beauty, but deny'd the Pelf
That buys your sex a Tyrant o'er itself.
The gen'rous God, who Wit and Gold refines,
And ripens Spirit as he ripens Mines,[66]   290
Kept Dross for Duchesses, the world shall know it,
To you gave Sense, Good-humour, and a Poet.

EPISTLE III

To ALLEN *Lord* BATHURST

ARGUMENT[1]

Of the Use *of* RICHES

THAT *it is known to few, most falling into one of the extremes,* Avarice *or* Profusion, v. 1, &c. *The Point discuss'd, whether the invention of Money has been more commodious, or pernicious to Mankind,* v. 21 to 78. *That Riches, either to the* Avaricious *or the* Prodigal, *cannot afford Happiness, scarcely Necessaries,* v. 81 to 108. *That Avarice is an absolute Frenzy, without an End or Purpose,* v. 109 &c. *Conjectures about the Motives of Avaricious men,* v. 113 to 152. *That the conduct of men, with respect to Riches, can only be accounted for by the* ORDER OF PROVIDENCE, *which works the general Good out of Extremes, and brings all to its great End by perpetual Resolutions,* v. 161 to 178. *How a* Miser *acts upon Principles which appear to him reasonable,* v. 179. *How a* Prodigal *does the same,* v. 199. *The due Medium, and true use of Riches,* v. 219. *The* Man of Ross, v. 250 [252]. *The fate of the* Profuse *and the* Covetous, *in two examples; both miserable in Life and in Death,* v. 301 [299] &c. *The Story of Sir* Balaam, v. 341 [339] to the end.

EPISTLE III

To ALLEN *Lord* BATHURST[2]

Who shall decide, when Doctors[3] disagree,
And soundest Casuists doubt, like you and me?
You hold the word, from Jove to Momus[4] giv'n,
That Man was made the standing jest of Heav'n;
And Gold but sent to keep the fools in play,   5
For some to heap, and some to throw away.
　　But I, who think more highly of our kind,
(And surely Heav'n and I are of a mind)
Opine, that Nature, as in duty bound,
Deep hid the shining mischief under ground: 10
But when by Man's audacious labour won,
Flam'd forth this rival to, its Sire, the Sun,[5]
Then careful Heav'n supply'd two sorts of Men,
To squander These, and Those to hide agen.
　　Like Doctors thus, when much dispute has past,   15
We find our tenets just the same at last.
Both fairly owning, Riches, in effect,
No grace of Heav'n or token of th' Elect;
Giv'n to the Fool, the Mad, the Vain, the Evil,
To Ward, to Waters, Chartres, and the Devil.[6]   20
What Nature wants, commodious Gold bestows,
'Tis thus we eat the bread another sows.
But how unequal it bestows, observe,
'Tis thus we riot, while, who sow it, starve:
What Nature wants (a phrase I much distrust)   25
Extends to Luxury, extends to Lust:
[And if we count among the Needs of life
Another's Toil, why not another's Wife?][7]
Useful, I grant, it serves what life requires,[8]
But dreadful too, the dark Assassin hires: 30
Trade it may help, Society extend;

114

But lures the Pyrate, and corrupts the Friend:
It raises Armies in a Nation's aid,
But bribes a Senate, and the Land's betray'd.[9]
   Oh! that such bulky Bribes as all might see,   35
Still, as of old, incumber'd Villainy!
In vain may Heroes fight, and Patriots[10] rave;
If secret Gold sap[11] on from knave to knave.
Could France or Rome[12] divert our brave designs,
With all their brandies or with all their wines?   40
What could they more than Knights and Squires
     confound,
Or water all the Quorum[13] ten miles round?
A statesman's slumbers how this speech would spoil![14]
"Sir, Spain has sent a thousand jars of oil;
"Huge bales of British cloth blockade the door;   45
"A hundred oxen at your levee roar."[15]
   Poor Avarice one torment more would find;
Nor could Profusion squander all in kind.
Astride his cheese Sir Morgan[16] might we meet;
And Worldly[17] crying coals from street to street,   50
Whom with a wig so wild, and mien so maz'd,
Pity mistakes for some poor tradesman craz'd.
Had Colepepper's[18] whole wealth been hops and hogs,
Could he himself have sent it to the dogs?
His Grace[19] will game: to White's[20] a Bull be led,   55
With spurning heels and with a butting head.[21]
To White's be carry'd, as to ancient games,
Fair Coursers, Vases, and alluring Dames.
Shall then Uxorio,[22] if the stakes he sweep,
Bear home six Whores, and make his Lady weep?   60
Or soft Adonis,[23] so perfum'd and fine,
Drive to St. James's a whole herd of swine?
Oh filthy check on all industrious skill,
To spoil the nation's last great trade, Quadrille![24]
   Once, we confess, beneath the Patriot's[25] cloak,   65

From the crack'd bag the dropping Guinea spoke,
And gingling down the back-stairs, told the crew,
"Old Cato is as great a rogue as you."[26]
Blest paper-credit! last and best supply!
That lends Corruption lighter wings to fly!   70
Gold imp'd[27] by thee, can compass hardest things,
Can pocket States, can fetch or carry Kings;[28]
A single leaf shall waft an Army o'er,
Or ship off Senates to a distant Shore;[29]
A leaf, like Sibyl's,[30] scatter to and fro   75
Our fates and fortunes, as the winds shall blow:
Pregnant with thousands flits the Scrap unseen,
And silent sells a King, or buys a Queen.[31]
    Well then, since with the world we stand or fall,
Come take it as we find it, gold and all![32]   80
    What Riches give us let us then enquire:
Meat, Fire, and Cloaths. What more? Meat, Cloaths,
        and Fire.[33]
Is this too little? would you more than live?
Alas! 'tis more than Turner[34] finds they give.
Alas! 'tis more than (all his Visions past)   85
Unhappy Wharton,[35] waking, found at last!
What can they give? to dying Hopkins,[36] Heirs;
To Chartres, Vigour; Japhet, Nose and Ears?[37]
Can they, in gems bid pallid Hippia[38] glow,
In Fulvia's[39] buckle ease the throbs below;   90
Or heal, old Narses,[40] thy obscener ail,
With all th' embroid'ry plaister'd at thy tail?
They might (were Harpax[41] not too wise to spend)
Give Harpax self the blessing of a Friend;
Or find some Doctor[42] that would save the life   95
Of wretched Shylock,[43] spite of Shylock's Wife:
But thousands die, without or this or that,
Die, and endow a College, or a Cat.[44]
To some, indeed, Heav'n grants the happier fate,

T" enrich a Bastard, or a Son they hate.[45]   100
   Perhaps you think the Poor might have their part?
Bond damns the Poor, and hates them from his heart:[46]
The grave Sir Gilbert holds it for a rule,
That "ev'ry man in want is knave or fool:"[47]
"God cannot love (says Blunt, with tearless eyes)   105
"The wretch he starves"—and piously denies:[48]
But the good Bishop, with a meeker air,
Admits, and leaves them, Providence's care.[49]
   Yet, to be just to these poor men of pelf,
Each does but hate his neighbour as himself: 110
Damn'd to the Mines, an equal fate betides
The Slave that digs it,[50] and the Slave that hides.
Who suffer thus, mere Charity should own,
Must act on motives pow'rful, tho' unknown.
Some War, some Plague, or Famine they foresee,   115
Some Revelation hid from you and me.
Why Shylock[51] wants a meal, the cause is found,
He thinks a Loaf will rise to fifty pound.
What made Directors cheat in South-sea year?
To live on Ven'son when it cost so dear.[52]   120
Ask you why Phryne the whole Auction buys?
Phryne foresees a general Excise.[53]
Why she and Sappho[54] raise that monstrous sum?
Alas! they fear a man will cost a plum.[55]
   Wise Peter[56] sees the World's respect for Gold,   125
And therefore hopes this Nation may be sold:
Glorious Ambition! Peter, swell thy store,
And be what Rome's great Didius[57] was before.
   The Crown of Poland, venal twice an age,[58]
To just three millions stinted modest Gage.   130
But nobler scenes Maria's dreams unfold,
Hereditary Realms, and worlds of Gold.
Congenial souls! whose life one Av'rice joins,
And one fate buries in th' Asturian Mines.[59]

Much injur'd Blunt![60] why bears he Britain's hate?   135
A wizard told him in these words our fate:
"At length Corruption, like a gen'ral flood,
"(So long by watchful Ministers withstood)
"Shall deluge all; and Av'rice creeping on,
"Spread like a low-born mist, and blot the Sun;   140
"Statesman and Patriot[61] ply alike the stocks,
"Peeress and Butler share alike the Box,[62]
"And Judges job, and Bishops bite the town,
"And mighty Dukes pack[63] cards for half a crown.
"See Britain sunk in lucre's sordid charms,   145
"And France reveng'd of Anne's and Edward's
          arms."[64]
'Twas no Court-badge, great Scriv'ner! fir'd thy brain,
No lordly Luxury, nor City Gain:
No, 'twas thy righteous end, asham'd to see
Senates degen'rate, Patriots[65] disagree,   150
And nobly wishing Party-rage to cease,
To buy both sides, and give thy Country peace.[66]
     "All this is madness," cries a sober sage:
But who, my friend, has reason in his rage?
"The ruling Passion, be it what it will,   155
"The ruling Passion conquers Reason still."[67]
Less mad the wildest whimsey we can frame,
Than ev'n that Passion, if it has no Aim;
For tho' such motives Folly you may call,
The Folly's greater to have none at all.[68]   160
     Hear then the truth: " 'Tis Heav'n each Passion sends,
"And diff'rent men directs to diff'rent ends.
"Extremes in Nature equal good produce,
"Extremes in Man concur to gen'ral use."[69]
Ask we what makes one keep, and one bestow?   165
That Pow'r who bids the Ocean ebb and flow,
Bids seed-time, harvest, equal course maintain,
Thro' reconcil'd extremes of drought and rain,

Builds Life on Death, on Change Duration founds,
And gives th' eternal wheels to know their rounds.[70]   170
   Riches, like insects, when conceal'd they lie,
Wait but for wings, and in their season fly.[71]
Who sees pale Mammon pine amidst his store,
Sees but a backward steward for the Poor;
This year a Reservoir, to keep and spare;   175
The next, a Fountain, spouting thro' his Heir,[72]
In lavish streams to quench a Country's thirst,
And men and dogs shall drink him till they burst.
   Old Cotta sham'd his fortune and his birth,[73]
Yet was not Cotta void of wit or worth: 180
What tho' (the use of barb'rous spits forgot)
His kitchen vy'd in coolness with his grot?[74]
His court with nettles, moats with cresses stor'd,
With soups unbought and sallads bless'd his board.[75]
If Cotta liv'd on pulse, it was no more   185
Then Bramins, Saints, and Sages did before;
To cram the Rich was prodigal expence,
And who would take the Poor from Providence?
Like some lone Chartreux[76] stands the good old Hall,
Silence without, and Fasts within the wall;   190
No rafter'd roofs with dance and tabor sound,
No noontide-bell invites the country round:
Tenants with sighs the smoakless tow'rs survey,
And turn th' unwilling steeds another way:
Benighted wanderers, the forest o'er,   195
Curse the sav'd candle, and unop'ning door;
While the gaunt mastiff growling at the gate,
Affrights the beggar whom he longs to eat.
   Not so his Son, he mark'd this oversight,[77]
And then mistook reverse of wrong for right.   200
(For what to shun will no great knowledge need,
But what to follow, is a task indeed.)
[Yet sure, of qualities deserving praise,

119

More go to ruin Fortunes, than to raise.][78]
What slaughter'd hecatombs,[79] what floods of wine,
Fill the capacious Squire, and deep Divine!
Yet no mean motive this profusion draws,   205
His oxen perish in his country's cause;
'Tis GEORGE and LIBERTY that crowns the cup,
And Zeal for that great House[80] which eats him up.
The Woods recede around the naked seat,
The Sylvans groan—no matter—for the Fleet: 210
Next goes his Wool—to clothe our valiant bands,
Last, for his Country's love, he sells his Lands.
To town he comes, completes the nation's hope,
And heads the bold Train-bands, and burns a Pope.[81]
And shall not Britain now reward his toils,   215
Britain, that pays her Patriots with her Spoils?
In vain at Court the bankrupt pleads his cause,
His thankless Country leaves him to her Laws.[82]
    The Sense to value Riches, with the Art
T' enjoy them, and the Virtue to impart,   220
Not meanly, nor ambitiously pursu'd,
Not sunk by sloth, nor rais'd by servitude;
To balance Fortune by a just expence,
Join with Œconomy, Magnificence;
With Splendour, Charity; with Plenty, Health;   225
Oh teach us, BATHURST! yet unspoil'd by wealth!
That secret rare, between th' extremes to move
Of mad Good-nature, and of mean Self-love.[83]
    To Worth or Want well-weigh'd, be Bounty giv'n,
And ease, or emulate, the care of Heav'n;[84]   230
(Whose measure full o'erflows on human race)
Mend Fortune's fault, and justify her grace.
Wealth in the gross is death, but life diffus'd;
As Poison heals, in just proportion us'd:
In heaps, like Ambergrise, a stink it lies,   235
But well-dispers'd, is Incense to the Skies.

Who starves by Nobles, or with Nobles eats?
The Wretch that trusts them, and the Rogue that cheats.
Is there a Lord, who knows a chearful noon
Without a Fiddler, Flatt'rer, or Buffoon?[85]   240
Whose table, Wit or modest Merit share,
Un-elbow'd by a Gamester, Pimp, or Play'r?
Who copies Your's, or OXFORD's[86] better part,
To ease th' oppress'd, and raise the sinking heart?
Where-e'er he shines, oh Fortune, gild the scene,   245
And Angels guard him in the golden Mean![87]
There, English Bounty yet a while may stand,
And Honour linger e'er it leaves the land.
    But all our praises why should Lords engross?
Rise, honest Muse! and sing the MAN of Ross:[88]   250
Pleased Vaga[89] echoes thro' her winding bounds,
And rapid Severn hoarse applause resounds.
Who hung with woods yon mountain's sultry brow?[90]
From the dry rock who bade the waters flow?[91]
Not to the skies in useless columns tost,   255
Or in proud falls magnificently lost,
But clear and artless, pouring thro' the plain
Health to the sick, and solace to the swain.
Whose Cause-way parts the vale with shady rows?
Whose Seats the weary Traveller repose?   260
Who taught that heav'n-directed spire to rise?
"The MAN of Ross," each lisping babe replies.
Behold the Market-place with poor o'erspread!
The MAN of Ross divides the weekly bread:
He feeds yon Alms-house, neat, but void of state,   265
Where Age and Want sit smiling at the gate:
Him portion'd maids, apprentic'd orphans blest,
The young who labour, and the old who rest.
Is any sick? the MAN of Ross relieves.
Prescribes, attends, the med'cine makes, and gives.   270
Is there a variance; enter but his door,

Balk'd are the Courts, and contest is no more.
Despairing Quacks with curses fled the place,
And vile Attorneys, now an useless race.
    "Thrice happy man! enabled to pursue   275
"What all so wish, but want the pow'r to do!
"Oh say, what sums that gen'rous hand supply?
"What mines, to swell that boundless charity?"
    Of Debts and Taxes, Wife and Children clear,
This man possest—five hundred pounds a year.   280
Blush, Grandeur, blush! proud Courts, withdraw your
        blaze!
Ye little Stars! hide your diminish'd rays.
    "And what? no monument, inscription, stone?
"His race, his form, his name almost unknown?"
Who builds a Church to God, and not to Fame,   285
Will never mark the marble with his Name:[92]
Go, search it there, where to be born and die,
Of rich and poor makes all the history;[93]
Enough, that Virtue fill'd the space between;
Prov'd, by the ends of being, to have been.   290
When Hopkins[94] dies, a thousand lights attend
The wretch, who living sav'd a candle's end:
Should'ring God's altar a vile image stands,[95]
Belies his features, nay extends his hands;
That live-long wig which Gorgon's self might own, 295
Eternal buckle takes in Parian stone.[96]
Behold what blessings Wealth to life can lend!
And see, what comfort it affords our end.
    In the worst inn's worst room, with mat half hung,[97]
The floors of plaister, and the walls of dung,   300
On once a flock-bed, but repair'd with straw,
With tape-ty'd curtains, never meant to draw,
The George and Garter dangling from that bed
Where tawdry yellow strove with dirty red,

Great Villers lies—alas! how chang'd from him,   305
That life of pleasure, and that soul of whim!
Gallant and gay, in Cliveden's proud alcove,[98]
The bow'r of wanton Shrewsbury[99] and love;
Or just as gay, at Council, in a ring
Of mimick'd Statesmen, and their merry King.   310
No Wit to flatter, left of all his store!
No Fool to laugh at, which he valu'd more.
There, Victor of his health, of fortune, friends,
And fame; this lord of useless thousands ends.

   His Grace's fate sage Cutler[100] could foresee,   315
And well (he thought) advis'd him, "Live like me."
As well his Grace reply'd, "Like you, Sir John?
"That I can do, when all I have is gone."
Resolve me, Reason, which of these is worse,
Want with a full, or with an empty purse?   320
Thy life more wretched, Cutler, was confess'd,
Arise, and tell me, was thy death more bless'd?
Cutler saw tenants break, and houses fall,
For very want; he could not build a wall.
His only daughter in a stranger's pow'r,   325
For very want; he could not pay a dow'r.
A few grey hairs his rev'rend temples crown'd,
'Twas very want that sold them for two pound.
What ev'n deny'd a cordial at his end,
Banish'd the doctor,[101] and expell'd the friend?   330
What but a want, which you perhaps think mad,
Yet numbers feel, the want of what he had!
Cutler and Brutus, dying both exclaim,
"Virtue! and Wealth! what are ye but a name!"

   Say, for such worth are other worlds prepar'd?   335
Or are they both,[102] in this their own reward?
That knotty point, my Lord, shall I discuss,
Or tell a Tale?—A Tale—it follows thus.[103]

   Where London's column, pointing at the skies,

Like a tall bully, lifts the head, and lyes;[104]   340
There dwelt a Citizen of sober fame,
A plain good man, and Balaam[105] was his name;
Religious, punctual, frugal, and so forth;
His word would pass for more than he was worth.
One solid dish his week-day meal affords,   345
An added pudding solemniz'd the Lord's:
Constant at Church, and Change; his gains were sure,
His givings rare, save farthings to the poor.
    The Devil was piqu'd such saintship to behold,
And long'd to tempt him like good Job of old: 350
But Satan now is wiser than of yore,
And tempts by making rich, not making poor.
    Rouz'd by the Prince of Air, the whirlwinds sweep
The surge, and plunge his Father in the deep;
Then full against his Cornish lands they roar,   355
And two rich ship-wrecks bless the lucky shore.[106]
    Sir Balaam now, he lives like other folks,
He takes his chirping[107] pint, and cracks his jokes:
"Live like yourself," was soon my Lady's word;
And lo! two puddings smoaked upon the board.   360
    Asleep and naked as an Indian lay,
An honest factor stole a Gem away:
He pledg'd it to the knight; the knight had wit,
So kept the Di'mond, and the rogue was bit.[108]
Some scruple rose, but thus he eas'd his thought,   365
"I'll now give six-pence where I gave a groat;
"Where once I went to church, I'll now go twice—
"And am so clear too of all other vice."
    The Tempter saw his time; the work he ply'd;
Stocks and Subscriptions pour on ev'ry side,   370
'Till all the Dæmon makes his full descent
In one abundant show'r of Cent per Cent,
Sinks deep within him, and possesses whole,
Then dubs Director, and secures his soul.[109]

Behold Sir Balaam, now a man of spirit,   375
Ascribes his gettings to his parts and merit;
What late he call'd a Blessing, now was Wit,
And God's good Providence, a lucky Hit.
Things change their titles, as our manners turn:
His Compting-house employ'd the Sunday-morn;[110]   380
Seldom at Church ('twas such a busy life)
But duly sent his family and wife.
There (so the Dev'l ordain'd) one Christmas-tide
My good old Lady catch'd a cold, and dy'd.
   A Nymph of Quality admires our Knight;   385
He marries, bows at Court, and grows polite:
Leaves the dull Cits, and joins (to please the fair)
The well-bred cuckolds in St. James's air:[111]
First, for his Son a gay Commission buys,
Who drinks, whores, fights, and in a duel dies: 390
His daughter flaunts[112] a Viscount's tawdry wife;
She bears a Coronet and P—x for life.
In Britain's Senate he a seat obtains,
And one more Pensioner St. Stephen gains.[113]
My Lady falls to play; so bad her chance,   395
He must repair it; takes a bribe from France;
The House impeach him; Coningsby[114] harangues;
The Court forsake him, and Sir Balaam hangs:
Wife, son, and daughter, Satan! are thy own,
His wealth, yet dearer, forfeit to the Crown: 400
The Devil and the King divide the prize,
And sad Sir Balaam curses God and dies.[115]

EPISTLE IV

TO

Richard Boyle, Earl of *Burlington*

ARGUMENT[1]

Of the Use of RICHES

The Vanity of Expence in People of Wealth and Quality. The abuse of the word Taste, v 13. *That the first principle and foundation, in this as in every thing else, is* Good Sense, v. 40. *The chief proof of it is to follow* Nature, *even in works of mere Luxury and Elegance. Instanced in* Architecture *and* Gardening, *where all must be adapted to the* Genius *and* Use *of the* Place, *and the Beauties not forced into it, but resulting from it,* v 50. *How men are disappointed in their most expensive undertakings, for want of this true Foundation, without which nothing can please* long, *if* at all; *and the best* Examples *and* Rules *will but be perverted into something* burdensome *or ridiculous,* v 65, &c. to 92. *A description of the* false Taste *of* Magnificence; *the first grand Error of which is to imagine that* Greatness *consists in the* Size *and* Dimension, *instead of the* Proportion *and* Harmony *of the whole,* v 97. *and the second, either in joining together* Parts incoherent, *or too* minutely resembling, *or in the* Repetition *of the same too frequently,* v 105, &c. *A word or two of false Taste in* Books, *in* Music, *in* Painting, *even in* Preaching *and* Prayer, *and lastly in* Entertainments, v 133, &c. *Yet* PROVIDENCE *is justified in giving Wealth to be squandered in this manner, since it is dispersed to the Poor and Laborious part of mankind,* v 169 (*recurring to what is laid down in the first book,* [*Essay*

127

on Man], Ep. ii. and in the Epistle preceding this, v 159 [161],
&c.) What are the proper Objects of Magnificence, and a
proper field for the Expence of Great Men, v 177, &c. and
finally, the Great and Public Works which become a Prince,
v 191, to the end.

EPISTLE IV²

To Richard Boyle, Earl of Burlington³

'Tis strange, the Miser should his Cares employ
To gain those Riches he can ne'er enjoy:
Is it less strange, the Prodigal should wast
His wealth, to purchase what he ne'er can taste?
Not for himself he sees, or hears, or eats;   5
Artists must chuse his Pictures, Music, Meats:
He buys for Topham,⁴ Drawings and Designs,
For Pembroke⁵ Statues, dirty Gods, and Coins;
Rare monkish Manuscripts for Hearne⁶ alone,
And Books for Mead, and Butterflies for Sloane.⁷   10
Think we all these are for himself? no more
Than his fine Wife, alas! or finer Whore.
      For what has Virro⁸ painted, built, and planted?
Only to show, how many Tastes he wanted.
What brought Sir Visto's ill got wealth to waste?   15
Some Dæmon whisper'd, "Visto! have a Taste."⁹
Heav'n visits with a Taste the wealthy fool,
And needs no Rod but Ripley with a Rule.¹⁰
See! sportive fate, to punish aukward pride,
Bids Bubo¹¹ build, and sends him such a Guide: 20
A standing sermon, at each year's expence,
That never Coxcomb reach'd Magnificence!
      You show us, Rome was glorious, not profuse,¹²
And pompous buildings once were things of Use.
Yet shall (my Lord) your just, your noble rules   25
Fill half the land with Imitating-Fools;¹³
Who random drawings from your sheets shall take,
And of one beauty many blunders make;¹⁴
Load some vain Church with old Theatric state,
Turn Arcs of triumph to a Garden-gate;¹⁵   30

129

Reverse your Ornaments, and hang them all
On some patch'd dog-hole ek'd with ends of wall;[16]
Then clap four slices of Pilaster on't,
That, lac'd with bits of rustic,[17] makes a Front.
Shall call the winds thro' long arcades to roar,   35
Proud to catch cold at a Venetian door;[18]
Conscious they act a true Palladian part,
And if they starve, they starve by rules of art.
   Oft have you hinted to your brother Peer,[19]
A certain truth, which many buy too dear: 40
Something there is more needful than Expence,
And something previous ev'n to Taste—'tis Sense:
Good Sense, which only is the gift of Heav'n,
And tho' no Science, fairly worth the seven:[20]
A Light, which in yourself you must perceive;   45
Jones and Le Nôtre have it not to give.[21]
   To build, to plant, whatever you intend,
To rear the Column, or the Arch to bend,
To swell the Terras, or to sink the Grot;
In all, let Nature never be forgot.[22]   50
But treat the Goddess like a modest fair,
Nor over-dress, nor leave her wholly bare;
Let not each beauty ev'ry where be spy'd,
Where half the skill is decently to hide.
He gains all points, who pleasingly confounds,   55
Surprizes, varies, and conceals the Bounds.[23]
   Consult the Genius of the Place in all;
That tells the Waters or to rise, or fall;
Or helps th'ambitious Hill the heav'ns to scale,
Or scoops in circling theatres the Vale;   60
Calls in the Country, catches op'ning glades,
Joins willing woods, and varies shades from shades;
Now breaks or now directs, th' intending Lines;[24]
Paints as you plant, and, as you work, designs.
   Still follow sense, of ev'ry Art the Soul,   65

Parts answ'ring parts shall slide into a whole,[25]
Spontaneous beauties all around advance,
Start ev'n from Difficulty, strike from Chance;
Nature shall join you; Time shall make it grow
A Work to wonder at—perhaps a STOW.[26]   70
　　Without it, proud Versailles! thy glory falls;
And Nero's Terraces[27] desert their walls:
The vast Parterres a thousand hands shall make,
Lo! COBHAM comes, and floats them with a Lake:[28]
Or cut wide views thro' Mountains to the Plain,   75
You'll wish your hill or shelter'd seat again.
Ev'n in an ornament its place remark,
Nor in an Hermitage set Dr. Clarke.[29]
　　Behold Villario's[30] ten-years toil compleat;
His Quincunx darkens, his Espaliers meet;[31]   80
The Wood supports the Plain,[32] the parts unite,
And strength of Shade contends with strength of Light;
A waving Glow the bloomy beds display,
Blushing in bright diversities of day,[33]
With silver-quiv'ring rills mæander'd o'er—   85
Enjoy them, you! Villario can no more;
Tir'd of the scene Parterres and Fountains yield,
He finds at last he better likes a Field.[34]
　　Thro' his young Woods how pleas'd Sabinus[35] stray'd
Or sat delighted in the thick'ning shade,   90
With annual joy the red'ning shoots to greet,
Or see the stretching branches long to meet!
His Son's fine Taste an op'ner Vista loves,
Foe to the Dryads of his Father's groves;
One boundless Green, or flourish'd Carpet views,[36]   95
With all the mournful family of Yews;[37]
The thriving plants ignoble broomsticks made,
Now sweep those Alleys they were born to shade.
　　At Timon's[38] Villa let us pass a day,
Where all cry out, "What sums are thrown away!"   100

So proud, so grand; of that stupendous air,
Soft and Agreeable come never there.
Greatness, with Timon, dwells in such a draught
As brings all Brobdignag before your thought.
To compass this, his building is a Town,   105
His pond an Ocean, his parterre a Down:
 Who but must laugh, the Master when he sees,
A puny insect, shiv'ring at a breeze!
Lo, what huge heaps of littleness around!
The whole, a labour'd Quarry above ground.³⁹   110
Two Cupids squirt before: a Lake behind
Improves the keenness of the Northern wind.
His Gardens next your admiration call,
On ev'ry side you look, behold the Wall!
No pleasing Intricacies intervene,   115
No artful wildness to perplex the scene;
Grove nods at grove, each Alley has a brother,
And half the platform just reflects the other.⁴⁰
The suff'ring eye inverted Nature sees,
Trees cut to Statues, Statues thick as trees;   120
With here a Fountain, never to be play'd;
And there a Summer-house, that knows no shade;
Here Amphitrite⁴¹ sails thro' myrtle bow'rs;
There Gladiators fight, or die in flow'rs;⁴²
Un-water'd see the drooping sea-horse mourn,   125
And swallows roost in Nilus' dusty Urn.⁴³
  My Lord advances with majestic mien,
Smit with the mighty pleasure, to be seen:
But soft—by regular approach—not yet—
First thro' the length of yon hot Terrace sweat;   130
And when up ten steep slopes you've drag'd your thighs,
Just at his Study-door he'll bless your eyes.
  His Study! with what Authors is it stor'd?⁴⁴
In Books, not Authors, curious is my Lord;
To all their dated Backs he turns you round: 135

These Aldus printed, those Du Suëil has bound.[45]
Lo some are Vellom, and the rest as good
For all his Lordship knows, but they are Wood.
For Locke or Milton 'tis in vain to look,
These shelves admit not any modern book.   140
    And now the Chapel's silver bell you hear,
That summons you to all the Pride of Pray'r:
Light quirks of Music, broken and uneven,
Make the soul dance upon a Jig to Heav'n.[46]
On painted Cielings you devoutly stare,[47]   145
Where sprawl the Saints of Verrio or Laguerre,[48]
On gilded clouds in fair expansion lie,
And bring all Paradise before your eye.
To rest, the Cushion and soft Dean invite,
Who never mentions Hell to ears polite.[49]   150
    But hark! the chiming Clocks to dinner call;
A hundred footsteps scrape the marble Hall:
The rich Buffet well-colour'd Serpents grace,[50]
And gaping Tritons spew to wash your face.
Is this a dinner? this a Genial room?[51]   155
No, 'tis a Temple, and a Hecatomb.[52]
A solemn Sacrifice, perform'd in state,
You drink by measure, and to minutes eat.
So quick retires each flying course, you'd swear
Sancho's dread Doctor and his Wand were there.[53]   160
Between each Act the trembling salvers ring,
From soup to sweet-wine, and God bless the King.
In plenty starving, tantaliz'd in state,
And complaisantly help'd to all I hate,
Treated, caress'd, and tir'd, I take my leave,   165
Sick of his civil Pride from Morn to Eve;
I curse such lavish cost, and little skill,
And swear no Day was ever past so ill.
    Yet hence the Poor are cloath'd, the Hungry fed;[54]
Health to himself, and to his Infants bread   170

The Lab'rer bears: What his hard Heart denies,
His charitable Vanity supplies.
    Another age shall see the golden Ear
Imbrown the Slope, and nod on the Parterre,
Deep Harvests bury all his pride has plann'd,   175
And laughing Ceres re-assume the land.[55]
    Who then shall grace, or who improve the Soil?
Who plants like BATHURST, or who builds like BOYLE.[56]
'Tis Use alone that sanctifies Expence,
And Splendor borrows all her rays from Sense.   180
    His Father's Acres who enjoys in peace,
Or makes his Neighbours glad, if he encrease:
Whose chearful Tenants bless their yearly toil,
Yet to their Lord owe more than to the soil
Whose ample Lawns are not asham'd to feed   185
The milky heifer and deserving steed;[57]
Whose rising Forests, not for pride or show,
But future Buildings, future Navies, grow:
Let his plantations stretch from down to down,
First shade a Country, and then raise a Town.   190
    You too proceed! make falling Arts your care,[58]
Erect new wonders, and the old repair;
Jones and Palladio to themselves restore,[59]
And be whate'er Vitruvius[60] was before:
Till Kings call forth th' Ideas of your mind,[61]   195
(Proud to accomplish what such hands design'd,)
Bid Harbors open, public Ways extend,
Bid Temples, worthier of the God, ascend;
Bid the broad Arch the dang'rous Flood contain,
The Mole projected break the roaring Main;   200
Back to his bounds their subject Sea command,
And roll obedient Rivers thro' the Land:
These Honours, Peace to happy Britain brings,
These are Imperial Works, and worthy Kings.[62]

Notes To The Poems

LIST OF ABBREVIATIONS

The following abbreviations have been used in the notes:

Corr: *The Correspondence of Alexander Pope*, ed. George Sherburn. 5 vols. Oxford: The Clarendon Press, 1956.

EC: *The Works of Alexander Pope*, ed. Whitwell Elwin and William John Courthope. 10 vols. London: John Murray, 1871-1889, Vol. III.

Griffith: Reginald Harvey Griffith. *Alexander Pope: A Bibliography*. 2 vols. Austin: University of Texas Press, 1927. Vol. I, Part ii.

Hervey: John, Lord Hervey. *Memoirs of the Reign of George II*, ed. John Wilson Croker. 3 vols. London: Bickers and Son, 1884.

P: A note by Pope from the 1751 edition of his works.

Spence: Joseph Spence. *Anecdotes, Observations, and Characters of Books and Men*, ed. Samuel Weller Singer. London: W. H. Carpenter, 1820.

TE: *The Twickenham Edition of the Poems of Alexander Pope*, gen. ed. John Butt. 6 vols. London: Methuen and Co., Ltd., 1939-1954. Vol. III, Part ii, *Epistles to Several Persons (Moral Essays)*, ed. F. W. Bateson.

W: A note by Warburton from the 1751 edition of Pope's works.

1 Argument] This is the Argument of 1751, with some sentences re-arranged to correspond to Pope's original organization of the poem. The 1751 line numbers have been retained, but line numbers which conform to the present edition are added in square brackets. The name "Clodio," which Warburton inadvertently kept in the 1751 edition, has here been changed to "Wharton," an alteration which Pope himself made in the text in 1744.

2 Cobham] Sir Richard Temple, Viscount Cobham (1669?-1749), was a friend of Pope's and a distinguished soldier under Marlborough in the War of the Spanish Succession. A devoted Whig and advocate of the House of Hanover, Temple was created Viscount Cobham by George I in 1718, and he supported Walpole for many years. In 1733, however, he joined the Opposition Whigs on the issue of Walpole's Excise Bill (cf. *Ep. Bath.*, line 122 and note 53) and in protest against Walpole's protection of the South Sea Company. He remained in opposition, gained the favor of the Prince of Wales, and after the fall of Walpole's ministry in 1742 became a Field Marshal. The famous gardens on his estate at Stowe in Buckinghamshire were laid out by the landscape architect Charles Bridgeman (cf. *Ep. Burl.*, line 70 and notes 26 and 28).

3 passenger] "A passer by or through. A traveller (usu. on foot" (OED). "A traveller, one who is upon the road, a wayfarer" (Johnson's Dictionary).

4 Line 14] *Those* refers to *observations* (line 11). Pope means that general conclusions (*Maxims*) about human nature are drawn from abstract ideas (*Notions*); empirical observations, on the other hand, are largely guesswork. He goes on to elaborate the idea and to say that neither method by itself is wholly valid. *Notions* is Locke's word for complex ideas, derived not directly from sense experience but from the mind (cf. *Essay on Human Understanding*, II. 22. 2).

5 Line 31] This is the pre-1744 reading. In the 1751 edition the line reads, "Nor will Life's stream for Observation stay" (line 37), a change apparently introduced for the sake of Warburton's reconstruction of the poem.

6 Lines 15-34] These lines pretty well sum up the reasons of the neo-classic age for distrusting the individual and the accidental and searching instead for universal truth.

7 Lines 35-36] "The Philosopher may invent a *rational hypothesis* that shall account for the appearances he would investigate; and yet that *hypothesis* be all the while very wide of *truth* and the *nature of things*" (W).

8 adust] "*Med.* Characterized by dryness of the body, heat, thirst, burnt colour of the skin . . . (OED). In *The Dunciad*, II, 37, the plump James Moore Smythe is said to possess just the opposite complexion (cf. *Ep. Lady*, note 56).

9 Lines 59-60] "The atrabilaire complexion of Philip II. is well known, but not so well that he derived it from his father Charles V. whose

health, the historians of his life tell us, was frequently disordered by bilious fevers. But what the author meant principally to observe here was, that this humour made both these princes act contrary to their Character; Charles, who was an active man, when he retired into a Convent; Philip, who was a man of the closet, when he gave the battle of St. Quintin" (W).

10 Lines 61-70] Cf. *Im. Hor.*, Ep. ii. 2. 33-51.

11 Lines 75-76] Cf. Montaigne, "Of the inconsistency of our actions," *The Complete Essays of Montaigne*, transl. Donald M. Frame, 3 vols. (Garden City, N. Y.: Doubleday and Co., Inc., 1969), II, 1-2; and commentary, pp. 12-14 above.

12 Lines 83-84] The pre-1744 reading of this couplet is as follows:

The mighty Czar what mov'd to wed a punk?

The mighty Czar might answer, he was drunk.

"After the battle of Pharsalia, Caesar pursued his enemy to Alexandria, where being infatuated with the charms of Cleopatra, instead of pushing his advantages, and dispersing the relicks of the Pharsalian quarrel, having narrowly escaped the violence of an enraged people, he brought upon himself an unnecessary war, at a time his arms were wanted elsewhere" (W).

Caesar was not a heavy drinker. Pope may have been in need of a rhyme, and he was to rhyme *drunk* and *punk* again in *Im. Hor.*, Ep. i. 1. 61-62. The "mighty Czar" of the earlier reading was Peter the Great.

13 Crape, Lawn] Crape: "In the 18th c., 'a sort of thin worsted stuff of which the dress of the clergy is sometimes made' (Bailey)." (OED). Lawn: "A kind of fine linen, resembling cambric. . . . This fabric used for the sleeves of a bishop. Hence the dignity or office of a bishop" (OED). In both definitions OED cites this line as an illustration.

14 Lines 87-92] Cf. *Es. Crit.*, lines 420-423.

15 Lines 87-100] "The poet having done with the *Philosopher*, now turns to the *Man of the world*; whose *first* mistake is in supposing men's true *Characters may be known by their station*. This, tho' a mere mob-opinion, is the opinion in fashion, and cherished by the Mob of all ranks; therefore, tho' beneath the poet's reasoning, he thought it deserving of his ridicule; and the strongest was what he gives (from v. 134 to 141 [87-92]) a naked exposition of the fact; to which he has subjoined (from v. 140-149 [93-100]) an ironical apology, that, as Virtue is cultivated with infinitely more labour in Courts than in Cottages, it is but just to set an infinitely higher value on it; which, says he with much pleasantry, is most agreeable to all the fashionable ways of estimation. For why do the connoisseurs prefer the lively colour in a Gem before that in a Flower, but for its extreme rarity and difficulty of production?" (W)

Pope alludes in this passage to the old belief that gems were produced by the rays of the sun. Cf. *Ep. Lady*, lines 289-290 and note 65; *Ep. Bath.*, line 12 and note 5.

138

16 CHANDOS] James Brydges, first Duke of Chandos (1673-1744), owner of the luxurious estate Cannons, near Edgeware. It was Chandos whom Pope was maliciously accused of satirizing as "Timon" in *Ep. Burl.* Pope may here be trying to make amends.

17 Shylock] EC notes that "On a printed leaf of this Essay among the Warburton papers, Pope has crossed out 'Shylock,' and written over it the real name 'Selkirk,'" for whom see Epilogue to Satires, Dialogue i. 92 . . . and Moral Essays iii. 92, 94 [94, 96]." Selkirk is Charles Douglas, Earl of Selkirk (1663-1739), who is attacked again in *Ep. Sat.*, II, 62, 158. The "Shylock" of *Ep. Bath.*, line 96, is probably not Selkirk but Edward Wortley Montague, although Selkirk is once again "Shylock" in lines 117-118 of that poem. Pope often blends his characters in this way. Cf. *Ep. Bath.*, note 41.

18 Manly] The main character in Wycherley's comedy *The Plain Dealer* (1676). Manly, an embittered idealist, raves in the play at the cynicism and hypocrisy of fashionable society.

19 Umbra] If a real person is meant here, no identification has so far proved possible.

20 a Queen] Queen Caroline (1683-1737), formerly Princess of Anspach-Bayreuth, queen of George II. She acted as a go-between from Walpole to the King (cf. *Ep. Arb.*, lines 69-82). The pre-1744 reading of the line is "Who but detests th' endearments of Courtine." Cf. *Im. Donne*, IV, 89, for another comment on what Pope seems to have regarded as insincerity on Caroline's part.

21 Line 121] This compliment, according to Warton, was intended for Swift (EC).

22 "The meaning must be that *flat falsehood* is often, if unexpectedly, to be met with in the stupid" (TE). However, Pope said to Spence in May 1730, "That Openness really yᵉ highest piece of Dissimulation" (quoted in TE xxii, and in George Sherburn, "Pope at Work," *Essays on the Eighteenth Century Presented to David Nichol Smith* [Oxford: The Clarendon Press, 1945], p. 50). This statement makes possible a slightly different interpretation: the dull pursue their ends through simple, unsophisticated falsehood, whereas the cunning are able to employ truth itself for dishonest purposes. The distinction is that between blundering dishonesty and subtle dishonesty.

23 Line 129] Cf. *Im. Hor.*, Ep. i. 1. 136-137.

24 Hackney] EC notes, following Gilbert Wakefield, that candidates for Parliament from Middlesex were put into nomination at Hackney.

25 Whitehall] The royal palace of Whitehall at one time occupied most of the space between St. James's Park and the Thames, running east and west, and between Charing Cross and Westminster Abbey, running north and south. As early as the thirteenth century Hubert de Burgh, Earl of Kent, bequeathed his property there to the friars of the Order of St. Dominic, who sold it, in 1248, to Walter de

Grey, Archbishop of York. It continued to be the town house of the archbishops of York until it was acquired by Wolsey, and much rebuilt, in the reign of Henry VIII. Whitehall continued to be the principal royal residence through the reign of James II, but in the reign of William and Mary it fell into disuse. All that now remains of Whitehall is the great Banqueting Hall designed by Inigo Jones, from one of the windows of which Charles I stepped onto a scaffold for his execution.

26 Catius] Catius has not been identified. In Horace *Serm.* ii. 4, Catius is the gourmet who gives sage advice on cooking and dining as the chief secrets for a happy life.

27 Patritio] "Lord G--n" (W). This is Sidney, first Earl of Godolphin (c. 1645-1712). He was a favorite of Charles II, a Tory, and after the Revolution of 1688 a secret partisan of James II. A genius at finance, he held high office in the treasury through several reigns. He was converted to the Whig party by Marlborough; and his son, Francis Godolphin, married the duke's daughter Henrietta Churchill, the "Philomedé" of *Ep. Lady* (lines 69-87 and note 23). Godolphin was fond of gambling, especially horseracing and cockfighting.

28 Picquette] Piquet: "A cardgame played by two persons with a pack of 32 cards (the low cards from the two to the six being excluded)" (*OED*, which cites this line as an illustration).

29 New-market-fame] Newmarket is a town in Cambridgeshire, famous as a horseracing center since the time of James I. Cf. *Im. Hor.*, Ep. ii. 1. 143-144.

30 Triumphant Leaders . . . save a groat] These four lines are in all the pre-1744 editions and were intended as a slur on the avarice and chicanery of the Duke of Marlborough. They may also have been in the suppressed "deathbed" edition of 1744, for TE notes that leaf A4 of that edition is a cancel, and the lines would have appeared on that leaf. If so, they were withdrawn for good after the printing. Warburton gives them as a variant in 1751. They are not included in the line numbering of the present volume.

31 Line 146] "Charron was an admirer of Montagne [*sic*]; had contracted a strict friendship with him; and has transferred an infinite number of his thoughts into his famous book *De la Sagesse*; but his moderating every-where the extravagant Pyrrhonism of his friend, is the reason why the poet calls him *more sage Charron*" (W). Evidence of Pope's familiarity with Charron's *De la Sagesse* is inconclusive, but he may often have heard Bolingbroke express a preference for Charron over Montaigne. Since Charron, as Warburton's note suggests, is less skeptical than Montaigne, Pope's use of the phrase "more sage Charron" frees him from a possible charge of Pyrrhonism and, at the same time, permits both an indirect compliment to Bolingbroke and a punning allusion to Charron's title.

32 Otho] M. Salvius Otho (A.D. 32-69), a debauched and effeminate Roman politician, was a friend of Nero and shared many of his orgies.

When Nero demanded that Otho divorce his beautiful and lascivious wife, Poppaea Sabina, Otho refused and was exiled to Lusitania, a province which he governed creditably for ten years. After the suicide of Nero in A.D. 68, Otho aspired to the throne and was actually emperor from Jan. 15 to April 16, 69. He led his own troops against those of another aspirant, Vitellius, whose army had already proclaimed him (Vitellius) emperor. Otho was defeated at the battle of Bedriacum, in Cisalpine Gaul, and he afterward committed suicide.

33 Cromwell] Oliver Cromwell was the butt of many royalist jokes. He was somewhat ungainly in appearance, but he was not a buffoon.

34 Line 148] "Louis XI of France wore in his Hat a leaden image of the Virgin Mary, which when he swore by, he feared to break his oath" (P).

35 Line 149] "Philip Duke of Orleans, Regent of France in the minority of Louis XV, superstitious in judicial astrology, tho' an unbeliever in all religion" (W).

36 Lines 150-151] "Philip V of Spain, who, after renouncing the throne for Religion, resum'd it to gratify his Queen; and Victor Amadeus II. King of Sardinia, who resign'd the crown, and trying to reassume it, was imprisoned till his death" (P). Cf. *Ep. Bath.*, note 59.

37 Lines 152-153] "The Czarina [Anna Ivanovna], the King of France [Louis XV], the Pope [Clement XII] and the abovementioned King of Sardinia" (W). EC supplies the identifications.

38 Lines 154-157] "Having thus proved what he had proposed, the *premisses* naturally lead him into a moral reflexion, with which he concludes his *first part*, namely, that constancy is to be expected in no human character whatsoever, but to be found only in God and his Laws: That as to Man, he is not only perpetually shifting and varying, even while *within the verge* of his own nature; but is frequently flying out into each extreme both *above* and *below* it: Now associating in good earnest with the Brutes; and now again affecting the imaginary conversation of Angels (See *Essay on Man*, Ep. ii v. 8)" (W). For line 155, cf. *Ep. Lady*, Line 154.

39 Scoto] James Johnston (1655-1737) was a Whig, a Presbyterian, a cousin of Bishop Gilbert Burnet, and joint Secretary of State for Scotland between 1692 and 1696. In 1695 he energetically investigated the infamous Massacre of Glencoe. Two years later he was given a grant of £5000, paid from the rents of the nonjuring bishops of Scotland. The money came in the form of yearly tithes, which Johnston collected with great rapacity (DNB).

40 Lines 162-165] This passage was added in 1744.

41 Lines 166-167] Cf. *Ep. Bath.*, line 379.

42 RULING PASSION] Pope's most complete statement concerning the Ruling Passion is in the second epistle of the *Essay on Man*. See the introduction, pp. 15-22 above.

43 Women] Another hint that Pope is speaking in this poem about all mankind, not just the male sex. See the introduction, pp. 10-12 above.

44 Wharton] The life of Philip, first and last Duke of Wharton (1700-1731) is a tragic story of undeveloped talents and wasted opportunities. His grandfather, fourth Baron Wharton, was a staunch Parliamentarian in the Civil War and fought at the battle of Edge Hill (1642). His father, Thomas, fifth Baron and first Marquis of Wharton, was one of those influential in bringing about the Revolution of 1688 and the accession of William and Mary. Philip, at a very early age, displayed intelligence and a remarkable talent for oratory, together with a tendency to alcoholism and an uncontrolled passion for buffoonery and dissipation of every kind. When Pope's Jacobite friend Francis Atterbury, Bishop of Rochester, was on trial for treason before the House of Lords, young Wharton defended him in a speech so eloquent that it was talked about for years afterward as a marvel of oratorical skill. Wharton was then twenty-four. His promise was so great that when he was eighteen the dukedom of Wharton was created for him by George I, an almost unprecedented action.

Wharton had a villa at Twickenham, less than a mile from Pope's, and there his eccentric debaucheries apparently wrought havoc with the poet's peace of mind and his literary gatherings. In fact, Wharton's intimacy with Lady Mary Wortley Montagu became so notorious that Lady Mary ever afterward blamed jealousy of Wharton as the cause of Pope's enmity toward her.

Having frittered away a huge fortune and having shown himself a fanatical Jacobite, Wharton went to the Continent to place himself at the service of the Pretender. There he accepted from the Pretender the meaningless title of Duke of Northumberland and the equally meaningless Order of the Garter, and he became a Roman Catholic. However, his drunkenness and his emotional instability rendered him all but useless to the exiled prince, and his fortunes went steadily from bad to worse. After an almost incredible two years of cadging liquor and fleeing bill collectors all over France and Spain, Wharton was taken in, sick and destitute, by the Bernardine monks at the monastery of Poblet in Catalonia. There, on May 31, 1731, he perished in utter misery, and there his body was interred. All his titles became extinct at his death. Pope called him "Clodio" in the pre-1744 editions. Cf. *Ep. Lady,* note 20.

45 The Club] Wharton was president of a notorious group of profligates known as the Hell-fire Club, which was suppressed by royal decree in 1721.

46 Tully, Wilmot] Wilmot is John Wilmot, second Earl of Rochester (1647-1680), famous poet and rake of the Restoration period, who, like Wharton, sought the comforts of religion in his final illness. Tully, of course, is the great Roman orator M. Tullius Cicero (106-43 B.C.).

47 Line 202] Wharton broke his father's heart by marrying, at the age of fifteen, a girl far beneath him in social and economic position.

He treated her shabbily and held her personally responsible for the death of their only son from smallpox. The Marquis of Wharton survived his son's marriage by only six weeks.

48 Catiline] L. Sergius Catilina (108?-62 B.C.), the notorious Roman politician whose intrigues were exposed by Cicero in 63 B.C. His conspiracies are described by Sallust in the *Catiline* (*Bellum Catilinarium*).

49 Line 213] "The sister of Cato, and mother of Brutus" (W). Her name was Servilia, and she was the half-sister, not the sister, of Cato of Utica (95-46 B.C.). Their mother was Livia, sister of M. Livius Drusus. Servilia's father was Q. Servilius Caepio, Livia's second husband; Cato's was M. Porcius Cato, Livia's first husband. When Cato of Utica's parents died, he was brought up in the house of his (and Servilia's) uncle, Drusus, who was tribune of the plebs in 91 B.C. Servilia was reportedly the most beloved of all Caesar's mistresses. For a comment on Caesar's supposed amorousness, cf. Montaigne, *Essays*, II, 33 ("The Story of Spurina") and the introduction, pp. 21-22 above.

50 Scipio] P. Cornelius Scipio Africanus Major (234-183? B.C.), son of P. Cornelius Scipio, whose life he saved when the Romans were defeated by Hannibal at the battle of the river Ticinus (218 B.C.). He received the surname Africanus in recognition of his brilliant victory over Hannibal at Zamia Regia, in Numidia (202 B.C.), a battle which put an end to the second Punic War. His bravery and piety gained him the profound admiration and respect of his fellow citizens.

51 Lucullus] L. Licinius Lucullus Ponticus (110?-56? B.C.), who received the surname Ponticus in token of his victories over Mithridates VI, King of Pontus, from 74 to 67 B.C. Upon Lucullus' retirement in 63 B.C., he pursued a life of magnificent luxury on his estates at Rome and Tusculum. He was a generous patron of literature and is said to have introduced cherries into Italy from Asia. He died in a state of senility and was buried at his Tusculan villa.

52 this] The Ruling Passion.

53 Lines 228-233] Both EC and TE note that this passage refers to Lancelot Blackburne (1658-1743), Archbishop of York from 1724 to 1743. The accusation is apparently unfounded.

54 Lines 233-236] Both EC and TE note that this story appears in Athenaeus viii. 341, where the glutton is the poet Philoxenus, and that Pope may have found it in La Fontaine, "Le Glouton," or in a sermon by John Hales (1584-1656). The word *helluo* means "glutton, squanderer" in Latin. Cf. *Ep. Lady*, line 79 and note 25.

55 Lines 238-241] These lines were added in 1744.

56 Lines 242-247] "This story, as well as the others, is founded on fact, tho' the author had the goodness not to mention the names. Several attribute this in particular to a very celebrated Actress, who, in detestation of the thought of being buried in woollen, gave these

her last orders with her dying breath" (P). "Narcissa" is Mrs. Anne Oldfield (1683-1730), as EC and TE note, one of whose favorite roles was that of Narcissa in Cibber's *Love's Last Shift* (1696). The dead were required by law to be buried in English woolen rather than in foreign stuffs. Cf. *Im. Hor.*, Ep. ii. 1. 330-331; and *Sober Advice from Horace*, Serm. i. 2. 5

57 Lanesb'row] "An ancient Nobleman, who continued this practice long after his legs were disabled by the gout. Upon the death of Prince George of Denmark, he demanded an audience of the Queen, to advise her to preserve her health and dispel her grief by *Dancing*" (P). This is Sir James Lane, second Viscount Lanesborough (1650-1724).

58 Euclio] Euclio is the old Athenian miser in Plautus' *Aulularia*, in whose house a pot of gold has been buried. His counterpart in Pope's thoughts, if there was one, has not been identified.

59 Lines 262-265] TE notes that these lines are still inscribed on a pillar erected by Cobham's widow at Stowe.

1 Argument] The Argument was omitted from the 1751 edition. It has been supplied here from the small octavo edition of July 1735, printed for Lawton Gilliver (Griffith 389). The original line numbers cited in the Argument have been retained, but line numbers corresponding to those in the present volume are given in square brackets.

2 A LADY] Martha ("Patty") Blount (1690-1762), her brother Michael and her sister Teresa, belonged to a well-known family of Roman Catholic gentry. The Blounts were friendly with Pope's family as early as 1710. Pope's intimacy with Martha gave rise to ugly rumors, attributed by Pope to her sister Teresa, with whom he had quarreled. Reports of Martha's charms vary widely; but she had striking blue eyes and seems to have been quite as sensible and goodhumored as Pope describes her as being. Pope bequeathed to "Patty" Blount the sum of £1000, together with many of his books and household furnishings.

3 Lines 5-10] "Attitudes in which several ladies affected to be drawn, and sometimes one lady in them all—The poet's politeness and complaisance to the sex is observable in this instance, amongst others, that, whereas in the *Characters of Men* he has sometimes made use of real names, in the *Characters of Women* always fictitious" (P).

4 Arcadia's Countess] EC, following Croker, identifies this person as Anne Finch, Countess of Winchilsea (1661-1720), author of some pleasant nature poetry. TE prefers Margaret, only daughter and heiress of Sir Robert Sawyer, who in 1684 was married to Thomas Herbert, eighth Earl of Pembroke (1656-1733), a man of learning and a well-known collector of art objects (cf. *Ep. Burl.*, line 8 and note 5). A pastoral portrait of Margaret, Pembroke's first wife, by Jan van der Vaart (c. 1687) is reproduced in TE opposite p. 48. TE's conjecture seems the more likely.

5 Fannia] A woman of Minturnae who sheltered Marius there in 88 B.C. She was an adultress, but Marius had nevertheless compelled her husband to return her dowry.

6 Cecilia] Saint Cecilia, a wealthy Roman virgin and martyr, is patron saint of music. Her feast day is November 22. According to legend, she swore a vow of chastity which extended to her wedding night, but her husband, Valerian, was so impressed that he became converted to Christianity. Cecilia was martyred in A.D. 177. Her story forms the substance of the Second Nun's Tale in Chaucer.

7 romantic] "Fantastic, extravagant, quixotic; going beyond what is rational or practical" (*OED*). The synonym in Johnson's Dictionary is "wild."

8 Line 21] "Instances of contrarieties, given even from such Characters as are most strongly mark'd, and seemingly therefore most consistent: As, I. In the *Affected*, v. 21 &c" (P). "Rufa" has not been identified, but the name also appears in *Sober Advice from Horace*, Serm. i. 2. 29; the whole passage from *Sober Advice* (lines 27-34) invites comparison with the present epistle.

145

9 Lines 23-26] "This thought is expressed with great humour in the following stanza:

"Tho' Artimesia talks, by fits,
Of councils, classics, fathers, wits;
  Reads Malbranche, Boyle, and Locke:
Yet in some things, methinks, she fails,
'Twere well if she wou'd pare her nails,
And wear a cleaner smock." (W)

This anticipation of "Rufa" and "Sappho" appeared in 1727, in the Pope-Swift *Miscellanies, the Last Volume*.

10 Sappho] This, of course, is Pope's old adversary Lady Mary Wortley Montagu (1689-1762), who had been a friend of his but for whom he eventually conceived a bitter hatred. The reasons for this enmity are not clear: one theory is mentioned in *Ep. Cob.*, note 44; another is that Pope once proposed marriage to Lady Mary and was answered with hoots of derision. At all events, in 1733 Pope published his *Im. Hor.*, Sat. ii. 1, where Lady Mary is attacked (lines 83-84) in what Croker once called, not inaccurately, "the most brutal and indecent couplet ever printed". (Lord Hervey's *Memoirs*, I, xxxix). From then on, the fat was in the fire. Lady Mary, in association with Lord Hervey (cf. *Ep. Bath.*, line 61 and note 23), struck back, and Pope, in turn, satirized her many times thereafter: cf *Im. Hor.*, Sat. ii. 2. 49-60 (in which Lady Mary and her husband appear as "Avidien" and "his wife"); *Sober Advice from Horace*, Serm. i. 2. 2 (by name), 18 ("Fufidia"), 125 ("Lady M--"), 166 ("Montague"); *Ep. Arb.*, 101 and 369 ("Sappho"); *Im. Donne*, II, 6 ("Sappho"); *Dunciad*, II, 136 (by name; this line appeared in the earlier *Dunciad*, II, 128; and cf. III, 141-144); *Im. Hor.*, Ep. i. 1. 164 (by name); and *Ep. Sat.*, I, 15 ("Sappho"), 112 (unnamed); II, 20 (unnamed, but the allusion is identical to that in I, 112). Pope constantly gibes at Lady Mary's personal uncleanliness, which, despite her intelligence and good looks, was notorious.

11 Lines 29-40] Continued from note 8: "II. Contrarieties in the *Soft-natured*" (P).

12 Lines 35-36] Cf. *R. Lock*, iv, 68.

13 Lines 37-40] For a similar fickleness, cf. "Villario" in *Ep. Burl.*, lines 79-88 and note 34.

14 Lines 45-52] Continued from notes 8 and 11: "III. Contrarieties in the *Cunning* and *Artful*" (P). The passage is a paraphrase of the first six lines of Pope's *Sylvia, a Fragment*, published in the Pope-Swift *Miscellanies, the Last Volume* (1727), from which Pope had borrowed before (cf. notes 9, 16, 52).

15 Lines 51-52] "Her charms consisted in the singular turn of her vivacity; consequently the stronger she exerted this vivacity the more forceable must be her attraction. But the point, where it came to excess, would destroy all the delicacy, and expose all the coarseness of sensuality" (W).

16 Lines 53-68] "IV. [Contrarieties] In the *Whimsical*" (P). The Narcissa of line 53 is not the same as that in *Ep. Cob.*, line 247. Rather, she is made up from a paraphrase of the rest of the *Sylvia* poem alluded to in note 14 above. Cf. also note 52.

17 Taylor] Jeremy Taylor (1613-1667), Bishop of Down and Connor and subsequently Bishop of Dromore, was a noted Anglican divine and an eloquent preacher. Narcissa is probably reading Taylor's *Rule and Exercises of Holy Living* (1650) and *Rule and Exercises of Holy Dying* (1651), which went through many editions in the seventeenth and eighteenth centuries and are still read today for the elegance and metaphorical richness of their style.

18 Book of Martyrs] John Foxe (1516-1587), the famous English martyrologist, was born in Boston, Lincolnshire, and educated at Oxford. He advocated an extreme Protestant position in the Church of England and, in the reign of Mary I, joined the English Protestant refugees on the Continent. His *Actes and Monuments*, popularly known as the "Book of Martyrs," was written first in Latin, at Strasbourg, but published in English in 1563 and, greatly enlarged, in 1570. It is an attempt to elevate the Protestant martyrs to a position of venerability on a level with the saints of medieval Christendom, and at one time it commanded a great following among devout Anglicans. It is pious, passionate, tendentious, and huge.

19 Citron] Citron-water: "A drink made from brandy flavoured with c.- or lemon-peel" (*OED*, which cites this line as an illustration). Cf. *R. Lock*, iv. 69.

20 his Grace] Identified by EC and TE as the Duke of Wharton. Cf. *Ep. Cob.*, lines 180-209 and note 44.

21 Chartres] Francis Charteris (1675-1732), born at Amsfield in Scotland, was one of the most notorious scoundrels of the day. A member of an ancient and wealthy family, he served in Marlborough's army and soon gained a reputation as a sharper at cards and dice. To those of his brother-officers whom he had ruined in this way he would lend money at usurious rates of interest. He was court-martialed and drummed out of his regiment, although he subsequently was able to buy another commission and rose to the rank of colonel. He was as addicted to women as to gambling, and in 1830 was tried and convicted at the Old Bailey for perpetrating a rape upon a servant girl named Ann Bond. On condition that he settle an annuity upon Ann, he was pardoned by the Crown. Pope provides an extensive note on Charteris at line 20 of *Ep. Bath.* He attacks Charteris many times elsewhere: cf. *Im Hor.*, Sat. ii. 1. 4 and 89; *Im. Hor.*, Ep. i. 6. 120; *Ep. Sat.*, II, 186; *Im. Donne*, II, 36. Cf. also Swift's note to his "Verses on the Death of Dr. Swift, D.S.P.D.," line 189, where Charteris is again attacked; Charteris reappears at line 324 of that poem. For details of Charteris' career, see *The Newgate Calendar*, ed. Sandra Lee Kerman (New York: Capricorn Books, 1962), pp. 114-121, to which I am indebted for this account of Charteris' crimes.

22 Lines 61-68] These elements of Narcissa's character are reminiscent

of the inconsistencies of the Duke of Wharton; cf. note 20 and *Ep. Cob.*, note 44.

23 Lines 69-87] "V. [Contrarieties] in the *Lewd and Vicious*" (P). "Philomedé," whose character follows, is identified by EC as Henrietta Churchill (1681-1733), daughter of the Duke and Duchess of Marlborough and, after the death of her father in 1722, Duchess of Marlborough in her own right. Known affectionately as "Hariote" to her family, she married the son of the Earl of Godolphin in 1698, a match which gave the Marlboroughs much satisfaction; cf. *Ep. Cob.*, note 27. Her friendship with the poet Congreve created a number of unpleasant rumors; among other things, she erected a monument to Congreve in Westminster Abbey. TE is inclined to doubt that "Philomedé" is Henrietta.

24 Lines 77-78] "In the MS.
"In whose mad brain the mixt ideas roll
Of Tall-boy's breeches, and of Caesar's soul." (W)

Tall-boy is a low-comedy clown in *The Jovial Crew* (first acted at the Cock Pit in Drury Lane, 1641) by Richard Brome (1590-1652?), a comedy which long held the stage and which Pope could well have seen. "Charles" was a conventional name for a male servant, as "James" is now for a butler and as "Betty" is for a maidservant in *Ep. Cob.*, line 247, and *R. Lock*, i, 148.

25 Helluo] This is not the same "Helluo" as that in *Ep. Cob.*, line 236. This "Helluo" is more of a gourmet and less of a glutton. Neither has been identified.

26 Dunce] In view of the statements in lines 71 and 77-78, TE's suggestion (p. 54, fn.) that the Dunce is "Philomedé's" husband is somewhat perilous.

27 Lines 87-100] "VI. Contrarieties in the Witty and Refin'd" (P). EC identifies "Flavia" as Elizabeth, Lady Lechmere, an inveterate gambler who committed suicide in 1739, four years after the publication of this poem. TE hesitantly prefers Henrietta Churchill once again (cf. note 23), but advances the possibility that "Flavia" is purely fictitious.

28 Line 92] Lucretia, according to the famous legend, was the beautiful and virtuous wife of L. Tarquinius Collatinus. She was raped by her husband's cousin, Sextus Tarquinius, son of the Roman king L. Tarquinius Superbus. After revealing the attack, she stabbed herself to death. The incident supposedly led to the expulsion of the Tarquins by L. Junius Brutus and the establishment of the Roman republic. Cf. Gower, *Confessio Amantis*, Chaucer, *Legend of Good Women*, and Shakespeare, *Rape of Lucrece.*

Rosamonda is Rosamond Clifford, beautiful mistress of Henry II whom Henry kept concealed in a labyrinth at Woodstock and who was popularly, though erroneously, thought to have been poisoned by Henry's queen, Eleanor of Aquitaine. A ballad on the subject by

148

Thomas Deloney is in Percy's collection (Thomas Percy, *Reliques of Ancient English Poetry*, ed. Henry Wheatley, 3 vols. [London: George Allen and Unwin, Ltd., 1885] II, 154 ff.).

29 Line 101] Neither "Simo" nor his mate has been identified.

30 Lines 105-106] A reminiscence of "Narcissa," lines 53-68.

31 Line 107] "Her who affects to laugh out of *fashion*, and strives to disbelieve out of *fear*" (W).

EC, following Warton, identifies "her Grace" as Mary Churchill 1689-1751), younger sister of Henrietta Churchill (cf. notes 23, 27), who married the Duke of Montagu. TE notes Walpole's belief that Pope meant Henrietta. The matter is obscure.

32 Ratafie] Ratafia: "A cordial or liqueur flavoured with almonds or peach-, apricot-, or cherry-kernels" (OED).

33 Atossa] There are two candidates for the original of "Atossa," Sarah, Duchess of Marlborough (1660-1744), and Catharine, Duchess of Buckinghamshire (1682?-1743). Both were highly eccentric and given to passionate rages. The former, in the words of Macaulay, was "at war with her whole kind, at war with her own children and grandchildren, great indeed and rich, but valuing greatness and riches chiefly because they enabled her to brave public opinion and to indulge without restraint her hatred to the living and the dead" (*History of England*, Ch. VII). The other duchess was married to John Sheffield, third Earl of Mulgrave (1648-1721), politician, military man, and poet, who was created Duke of Buckingham and Normanby in 1703. She was the daughter of Catherine Sedley, mistress of James II, whose father, in turn, was Sir Charles Sedley, the Restoration rake and poet. It is quite likely, therefore, that the duchess may have been the natural daughter of James II. At any rate, the idea was an obsession with her, and in her later years she became insane, demanding all the honors and privileges of a princess of the blood royal.

It was long believed that the Duchess of Marlborough was "Atossa," but this identification may bave been publicized out of spite by Bolingbroke, who had learned after Pope's death that one of his works had been printed by the poet without his authorization. TE, in an appendix (Appendix A, pp. 155-164), examines the "Atossa" problem in great detail and makes a strong case for the Duchess of Buckinghamshire. EC prefers the Duchess of Marlborough, but straddles the fence. Samuel Johnson, like nearly all eighteenth-century commentators, assumed that the Duchess of Marlborough was "Atossa." The whole question is very difficult. The "Atossa" passage was reprinted separately in 1746 (Griffith 613) as "Verses Upon the Late D--ss of M-- -- -, By Mr. P- -."

34 Line 122] "After v. 122 in the MS.

"Oppres'd with wealth and wit, abundance sad!
One makes her poor, the other makes her mad." (W)

35 Line 148] "After v. 148 in the MS.

> "This Death decides, nor lets the blessing fall
> On any one she hates, but on them all.
> Curs'd chance! this only could afflict her more,
> If any part should wander to the poor." (W)

36 Line 150] "Alluding and referring to the great principle of his Philosophy, which he never loses sight of, and which teaches, that Providence is incessantly turning the evils arising from the follies and vices of men to general good" (W). This is a major theme of the *Essay on Man* and of *Ep. Bath*; cf. *Ep. Bath.*, note 72.

37 Line 154] Cf. *Ep. Cob.*, line 155.

38 Cloe] EC identifies "Cloe" as Henrietta (1681-1767), daughter of Sir Henry Hobart; wife of Charles Howard, Earl of Suffolk; and mistress of George II. TE points out, however, that Lady Suffolk was an intimate friend of Martha Blount, to whom this poem is addressed.

39 Lines 177-178 Both EC and TE print Warton's note: "He alludes to a particular circumstance. Pope being at dinner with her, heard her order her footman to put her in mind to send to know how Mrs. Blount, who was ill, had passed the night."

40 *Queen*] Queen Caroline (1683-1737), queen of George II.

41 Lines 181-186] Cf. *Ep. Cob.*, lines 87-96.

42 Lines 187-190] Cf. Swift, *A Tale of a Tub*, Section IX, "A Digression concerning the Original, the Use and Improvement of Madness in a Commonwealth," especially the famous passage on the woman whom the author says he saw flayed.

43 QUEENSBERRY] Catherine, Duchess of Queensberry (1700-1777), granddaughter of Edward Hyde, first Earl of Clarendon, and wife of Charles Douglas (1698-1778), third Duke of Queensberry and second Duke of Dover. A remarkably beautiful and eccentric woman, she was patroness and friend to many literary men—Thomson, Prior, Congreve, Pope, and especially Gay.

44 Line 198] "*Mah'met*, servant to the late King [George I], said to be the son of a Turkish Bassa, whom he took at the Siege of Buda, and constantly kept about his person" (P).

"Dr. *Stephen Hale*, not more estimable for his useful discoveries as a natural Philosopher, than for his exemplary Life and Pastoral Charity as a Parish Priest" (W). This is Dr. Stephen Hales (1637-1761), Vicar of Teddington, the famous physiologist and vivisectionist. Pope respected Hale's piety but deplored his interest in vivisection, as he told Spence about 1743 (Spence p. 293). The Hale in *Im. Hor.*, Ep. i. 1. 173, is Richard Hale (1670-1728), physician at Bedlam and a specialist in insanity.

45 Line 199] "In the former Editions, between this and the foregoing lines, a want of Connexion might be perceived, occasioned by the

omission of certain *Examples* and *Illustrations* to the Maxims laid down; and tho' some of these have since been found, viz. the Characters of *Philomede, Atossa, Cloe,* and some verses following, others are still wanting, nor can we answer that these are exactly inserted" (Pope's note, though it is not initialed in the 1751 edition). This curious statement seems to have obvious bearing on the failure of the three characters mentioned to appear in the pre-1744 editions and on the eventual suppression of the "deathbed" edition of 1744. TE notes (p. 39) that this is Pope's only public statement on the matter. Cf. TE's discussion, pp. 38-42.

> "After v. 198 in the MS.
>
>> "Fain I'd in Fulvia spy the tender Wife;
>> I cannot prove it on her, for my life:
>> And, for a noble pride, I blush no less.
>> Instead of Berenice, to think on Bess.
>> Thus while immortal Cibber only sings
>> (As * and H**y preach) for queens and kings,
>> The nymph, that ne'er read Milton's mighty line,
>> May, if she love, and merit verse, have mine." (W)

EC, following Croker, supplies for the asterisks Hare and Hoadley.

46 Line 203] "There is something particular in the turn of this assertion, as making their disguising in public the necessary effect of their being *bred to disguise;* but if we consider that female Education is an art of teaching not to *be,* but to *appear,* we shall have no reason to find fault with the exactness of the expression" (W). Cf. lines 285-299 and note 65.

47 Line 206] "For Women are taught Virtue so artificially, and Vice so naturally, that, in the nice exercise of them, they may be easily mistaken for one another" (SCRIB).

48 Line 207] "The former part having shewn, that the *particular Characters of Women* are more various than those of Men, it is nevertheless observed, that the *general* Characteristic of the sex, as to the *ruling Passion,* is more uniform" (P).

49 That] The love of pleasure.

50 Line 211] "This is occasioned partly by their *Nature,* partly by their *Education,* and in some degrees by *Necessity*" (P).

51 This] The love of sway.

52 Lines 215-216] In this couplet Pope echoes for the third time his *Sylvia, A Fragment;* cf. notes 14, 16. EC compares *Spectator,* No. 154.

53 Line 219] "What are the *Aims* and the *Fate* of this Sex? --I. As to *Power*" (P).

54 Line 231] "[What are the *Aims* and *Fate of this Sex?*]—II. As to *Pleasure*" (P).

151

55 Lines 241-242] EC and TE note that this couplet is adapted from an epigram by Pope in *Miscellaneous Poems by Several Hands, Publish'd by D. Lewis* (1730):

> When other fair ones to the shades go down,
> Still Chloe, Flavia, Delia stay in town:
> Those ghosts of beauty wandering here reside,
> And haunt the places where their honour died.

The version printed in TE is slightly different.

56 Lines 243-248] These lines of Pope's, slightly altered, had already been used by James Moore Smythe (probably with Pope's permission) in his comedy *The Rival Modes*, II, acted Jan 27, 1767 (N.S.). Somebody, probably Pope himself, then wrote a letter to the *Daily Journal* accusing Pope of plagiarism from Moore Smythe, whereupon Pope replied with a letter accusing Moore Smythe of plagiarism from him. The whole matter is discussed in an extensive note by Pope to *Dunciad*, II, 35-50, a devastating satire on Moore Smythe. Cf. also *Ep. Cob.*, note 8.

57 Line 249] "Advice for their true Interest" (P).

58 the Ring] The Ring was a group of trees near the Serpentine in Hyde Park. Londoners of fashion had been fond of driving their carriages around it since the reign of Charles I.

59 Lines 253-256] EC and TE note the origin of these lines in the *Lines to Erinna* (1722), in which Pope compliments Judith Cowper on her "virgin modesty." Judith was William Cowper's aunt.

60 Codille] "A term used at ombre when the game is lost by the player who challenges to win it" (*OED*). To "lose the codille" is roughly the equivalent of being "set" in contract bridge. Cf. R. *Lock*, iii, 91-92. There is a description of the game of ombre in TE, III, 361-368.

61 Small-pox] Martha Blount herself was disfigured by smallpox.

62 Lines 265-268] Cf. R. *Lock*, iii, 157-160.

63 Lines 269-280] The following is Pope's original note, taken from the small octavo edition of July 1735 (Griffith 389) II, 20: "The Picture of an esteemable Woman, with the best kind of Contrarieties." For the 1751 edition Warburton, who disliked Martha Blount and wished to make it seem that the portrait was not a specific compliment to her, added the following qualification: ". . . created out of the poet's imagination; who therefore feigned those circumstances of a *Husband*, a *Daughter*, and love for a *Sister*, to prevent her being mistaken for any of his acquaintance. And having thus made his *Woman*, he did, as the ancient poets were wont, when they had made their *Muse*, invoke, and address his poem to, her."

64 Line 283] The year was 1690. For a similar bit of gallantry, cf. Swift's poem "On Stella's Birthday (1718-1719)."

65 Lines 285-292] "The poet concludes his Epistle with a fine *Moral*, that deserves the serious attention of the public: It is this, that all the extravagances of these *vicious* Characters here described, are much inflamed by a wrong Education, hinted at in v. 203 [cf. note 46]; and that even the *best* are rather secured by a *good natural* than by the prudence and providence of parents; which observation is conveyed under the sublime classical machinery of Phoebus in the ascendant, watching the natal hour of his favourite, and averting the ill effects of her parents mistaken fondness: For Phoebus, as the god of Wit, confers Genius; and, as one of the astronomical influences, defeats the adventitious byas of education.

"In conclusion, the great Moral from both these Epistles together is, that the two rarest things in all Nature are a DISINTERESTED MAN, and a REASONABLE WOMAN" (W). Cf. *Im. Hor.*, Ep. ii. 2. 278-279.

66 Lines 289-290] This refers to the common belief that gold and precious stones were created by the sun's rays. Cf. *Ep. Cob.*, note 15, and *Ep. Bath.*, note 5.

1 Argument] This is the Argument of the 1751 edition, except that the sequence of ideas, as in *Ep. Cob.*, has been slightly altered to fit Pope's original organization. Original line numbers have been kept, but those which pertain to the present edition are given in square brackets. The pronoun *it* in the first sentence refers to the use of riches.

2 BATHURST] Allen Bathurst, first Earl Bathurst (1684-1775), belonged to an ancient Saxon family. He was a devoted Tory and, like the Duke of Wharton, defended Atterbury in the House of Lords in May 1723. He was a friend of Pope's and of such literary men as Congreve, Prior, and Sterne. The last named, in his third Letter to Eliza, comments admiringly on Bathurst's wit and haleness at the age of eighty-five.

3 Doctors] In this often-quoted line Pope does not mean physicians, as is popularly supposed, but scholars, schoolmen in the medieval sense. Cf. line 15. In lines 95 and 330, however, he seems to mean a physician. Cf. *Im. Hor.*, Ep. i. 1. 23-24.

4 Momus] In Greek mythology, the god of jeering criticism, called by Hesiod the son of primeval Night. At the end of Sidney's *Defence of Poesie* there is a pun on *Momus* and *mome*, an old word for a blockhead. *Mome* is in Johnson's Dictionary.

5 Line 12] Another allusion to the belief that gold and precious stones were nurtured by the sun. Cf. *Ep. Cob.*, note 15, and *Ep. Lady*, note 65.

6 Line 20] "JOHN WARD, of Hackney, Esq.; Member of Parliament, being prosecuted by the Duchess of Buckingham, and convicted of Forgery, was first expelled the House, and then stood in the Pillory on the 17th of March 1727. He was suspected of joining in a conveyance with Sir John Blunt, to secrete fifty thousand pounds of that Director's Estate, forfeited to the South Sea Company by Act of Parliament. The Company recovered the fifty thousand pounds against Ward; but he set up prior conveyances of his real estate to his brother and son, and conceal'd all his personal, which was computed to be one hundred and fifty thousand pounds: These conveyances being also set aside by a bill in Chancery, Ward was imprisoned, and hazarded the forfeiture of his life, by not giving in his effects till the last day, which was that of his examination. During his confinement, his amusement was to give poison to dogs and cats, and see them expire by slower or quicker torments. To sum up the *worth* of this gentleman, at the several aera's of his life; at his standing in the Pillory he was *worth above two hundred thousand pounds*; at his commitment to Prison, he was *worth one hundred and fifty thousand*, but has been since so far diminished in his reputation, as to be thought a *worse man* by *fifty or sixty thousand*.

"FR. CHARTRES, a man infamous for all manner of vices. When he was an ensign in the army he was drumm'd out of the regiment for a cheat; he was next banish'd Brussels, and drumm'd out of Ghent on the same account. After a hundred tricks at the gaming-tables, he took to lending of money at exorbitant interest and on great penalties, accumulating premium, interest, and capital into a new capital, and seizing to a minute when the payments became due; in a word, by a constant attention to the vices, wants, and follies of mankind, he acquired an immense fortune. His house was a perpetual bawdy-house. He was twice condemn'd for rapes, and pardoned: but the last time [for the rape of Ann Bond; cf. *Ep. Lady*, note 21] not without imprisonment in Newgate, and large confiscations. He died in Scotland in 1731 [*sic*], aged 62. The populace at his funeral rais'd a great riot, almost tore the body out of the coffin, and cast dead dogs, &c. into the grave along with it. The following Epitaph contains his character very justly drawn by Dr. Arbuthnot:

HERE continueth to rot
The Body of FRANCIS CHARTRES,
Who with an INFLEXIBLE CONSTANCY,
and INIMITABLE UNIFORMITY of life,
PERSISTED,
In spite of AGE and INFIRMITIES,
In the practice of EVERY HUMAN VICE;
Excepting PRODIGALITY and HYPOCRISY;
His insatiable AVARICE exempted him from the
first,
His matchless IMPUDENCE from the second.
Nor was he more singular
in the undeviating *Pravity* of his *Manners*
Than successful
in *accumulating* WEALTH.
For, without TRADE or PROFESSION,
Without TRUST of PUBLIC MONEY,
And without BRIBE-WORTHY Service,
He acquired, or more properly created,
A MINISTERIAL ESTATE.
He was the only Person of his Time,
Who cou'd CHEAT without the Mask of HONESTY,
Retain his Primeval MEANNESS
When possess'd of TEN THOUSAND a YEAR,
And having daily deserved the GIBBET for what
he *did*,
Was at last condemn'd to it for what he *could*
not *do*.
Oh Indignant Reader!
Think not his Life useless to Mankind!
PROVIDENCE conniv'd at his execrable Designs,
To give to After-ages
A conspicuous PROOF and EXAMPLE
Of how small Estimation is EXORBITANT WEALTH
in the sight of GOD,
By his bestowing it on the most UNWORTHY of
ALL MORTALS.

This Gentleman was *worth seven thousand pounds* a year estate in Land, and about *one hundred thousand in Money*.

"Mr. WATERS, the third of these worthies, was a man in no way resembling the former in his military, but extremely so in his civil capacity; his great fortune having been rais'd by the like diligent attendance on the necessities of others. But this gentleman's history must be deferred till his death, when his *worth* may be known more certainly" (P).

Ward, who died in 1755, is also noticed in *Dunciad*, III, 34, where Pope furnishes a condensed version of the above note, and *Ep. Sat.*, I, 119. The Ward mentioned in *Im. Hor.* Ep. i. 6. 56 and ii. 1. 182, is not John but the medical quack Joshua Ward. For Charteris, cf. *Ep. Lady*, note 21. Peter Walter (1664?-1746), whose name also appears as Walters and Waters, was a member of Parliament and a famous usurer, who left a fortune of some £300,000 at his death. He is Peter Pounce, the rascally steward, in Fielding's *Joseph Andrews*. Pope satirizes him again and again: *Im. Hor.*, Sat. ii. 1. 3; ii. 1. 40; Sat. ii. 2. 68; Ep. ii, 1. 197; *Im. Donne*, II, 65-78; *Ep. Sat.*, I, 10. 121; II, 56-60; and possibly *1740*, line 26 Cf. note 56.

7 Lines 27-28] These lines appear in all the pre-1744 editions but were suppressed by Warburton "for their bad reasoning," as he put it. TE includes them; EC relegates them to the notes. They seem too good to omit.

8 Lines 29-34] Warburton transformed these lines into a stichomythic dialogue between *P* and *B*.

9 Line 34] EC notes this as a stroke at the corruption of Walpole's administration. An instructive, though somewhat intemperate, comment on the subject is to be found in the Diary of John, Viscount Perceval and first Earl of Egmont (1683-1748). Speaking of Walpole, Lord Egmont writes, ". . . it is this meanness of his (the prostitution of the character of a first Minister in assisting and strenuously supporting the defence of dunghill worms, let their cause be ever so unjust, against men of honour, birth, and fortune, and that in person too), that gains him so much ill-will . . . Sir Robert, like the altars of refuge in old times, is the asylum of little unworthy wretches who, submitting to dirty work, endear themselves to him . . ." (*English Historical Documents*, David C. Douglas, gen. ed., 12 vols.; X, ed. D. B. Horn and Mary Ransome [New York: Oxford University Press, 1957], 127).

10 Patriots] "This appellation was generally given to those in opposition to the Court. Though, some of them (which our author hints at) had views too mean and interested to deserve that name" (Pope's note to *Ep. Sat.*, I, 24). Johnson's Dictionary notes that "It is sometimes used for a factious disturber of the government." Cf. line 65; cf. also Dryden, *Absalom and Architophel*, lines 965-968.

11 sap] "To make way in a stealthy or insidious manner" (OED), which cites this line as an illustration.

12 Rome] "The head-quarters of the Pretender's party. In the Chauncy
MS. the lines run:
"Much would it check sage F--s deep design,
Were France to pay her pensioners in wine.
F-- is of course Fleury" (EC). André Hercule Cardinal de Fleury
(1653-1743), French priest and statesman, was chief adviser to
Louis XV from 1726-1743. He was noted for his wisdom and his
devotion to peace. Cf. note 14.

13 Quorum] "A bench of justices" (Johnson's Dictionary).

14 Statesman] Pope may have had Fleury in mind once again; the
Huntington MS gives "Flxxy's deep Quiet" for "A Statesman's
slumbers." Cf. Wasserman, pp. 76-77, and note 12.

15 Lines 35-46] EC and TE, following Gilbert Wakefield, compare
"The Rapture," by John Sheffield, Earl of Mulgrave and Duke of
Buckingham and Normanby (cf. *Ep. Lady*, note 33). Mulgrave was
a friend of Dryden and later of Pope, who edited his works two
years after his death.

16 Line 49] EC and TE, following Wakefield, compare John Philips,
"The Splendid Shilling," lines 22-29, describing a Welshman ("a
Cambro-Britain") who
Upon a cargo of famed Cestrian cheese
High over-shadowing rides, with a design
To vend his wares . . .
Pope's "Sir Morgan," from his name, is clearly a Welshman.

17 Line 50] "Some Misers of great wealth, proprietors of the coal-mines,
had enter'd at this time into an association to keep up coals to
an extravagant price, whereby the poor were reduced almost to
starve, till one of them taking the advantage of underselling the
rest, defeated the design. One of these Misers was *worth ten
thousand*, another *seven thousand* a year" (P). EC and TE identify
"Worldly" as Edward Wortley Montagu (1681-1761), avaricious
husband of Pope's old enemy Lady Mary. Cf. *Im. Hor.*, Sat. ii. 2.
49; Ep. ii. 2. 234.

18 Colepepper] "Sir WILLIAM COLEPEPPER, Bart., a person of
an ancient family, and ample fortune, without one other quality
of a Gentleman, who, after ruining himself at the Gaming-table,
past the rest of his days in sitting there to see the ruin of others;
preferring to subsist upon borrowing and begging, rather than to
enter into any reputable method of life, and refusing a post in
the army which was offer'd him" (P). The name of Colepepper
(1668-1740) was the last of several to occupy this spot in Pope's
poem.

19 His Grace] Wriothesley Russell, third Duke of Bedford (1708-1732),
lost in one night's play at White's (cf. note 20) the sum of £3800.
The winner was Sir Henry Jansen (d. 1766); whose fondness for
the gaming tables at White's is mentioned in the same breath with

that of Colley Cibber in *Dunciad*, IV, 326. Cf. also *Im. Donne*, II, 88.

20 White's] White's Club, the famous gambling resort in St. James's Street, began in the 1690's as White's Chocolate House, whence issued those of the *Tatler* papers devoted to "gallantry, pleasure, and entertainment." The establishment soon developed into a gambling house, and the proprietors were compelled to turn it into a club to exclude the more offensive criminal element. Colley Cibber used to gamble at White's and was known there as "King Coll"; cf. *Dunciad* I, 203, 321. The place was destroyed by fire April 28, 1733, an incident depicted by Hogarth in Plate VI of *The Rake's Progress*. In Plate IV of the series, the exterior of White's is in the background, just on the point of being struck by lightning.

21 Lines 55-56] Cf. Vergil *Eclogues* 3. 135-136 (Dryden's translation). The shepherd Menalcas is speaking:

> My Pollio writes himself:—a bull be bred,
> With spurning heels, and with a butting head.

In the original:

> Pollio et ipse facit nova carmina: pascite taurum,
> iam cornu petat et pedibus qui spargat harenam.

22 Uxorio] John Hervey, first Earl of Bristol (1665-1751), was elevated to the peerage in 1703. He was a Whig and a supporter of the House of Hanover; he was also a learned man and a well-known gambler. The wife to whom Pope alludes in the next line is the second countess, by whom "Uxorio" had sixteen children. One of these is the "Adonis" of line 61.

23 Adonis] John Hervey, Baron Hervey of Ickworth (1696-1743), was the son of "Uxorio" (cf. note 22). As vice-chamberlain of the royal household, he had chambers in St. James's Palace. Pope detested Hervey for seasons not wholly clear—partly, no doubt, his effeminate appearance and behavior, partly his influence over George II's queen (cf. *Ep. Cob.*, note 20), and partly his intimacy with Lady Mary Wortley Montagu (cf. *Ep. Lady*, note 10), whom Pope at one time liked and may have loved. A poet of sorts, Hervey was probably co-author, with Lady Mary, of an attack on Pope as scurrilous as his on them. Pope satirized Hervey repeatedly: cf. *Im. Hor.*, Sat. ii. 1. 6 ("Lord Fanny"); Sat. ii. 2. 101 ("Lord Fanny"); *Ep.* ii. 1. 105-106 (not by name); *Im. Donne*, IV, 178 ("Fannius"); *Sober Advice from Horace*, Serm. i. 2. 2 ("Lord Fanny"), 30 ("Sweet *Moll* and *Jack*," for Lord and Lady Hervey), 92 ("Lord Fanny"); *Ep. Arb.*, 149 ("gentle Fanny"), 305-333 ("Sporus," the name of the youth whom, according to Suetonius, Nero castrated and then married), 363 ("Sporus"), 380 (the *Curll* of Court); *Ep. Sat.*, I, 50 ("Lord Fanny"), 71-72 ("H--vy"); *1740*, 57 (by name).

Despite lifelong ill health and widespread doubts concerning his manhood, Lord Hervey managed to sire eight children.

24 Quadrille] "A card game played by four persons with forty cards, the eights, nines, and tens of the ordinary pack being discarded"

(*OED*). According to the contemporary report of Sir Charles Hanbury Williams, Lord Hervey won large sums of money from the ladies at quadrille (cf. Romney Sedgwick [ed.], *Lord Hervey's Memoirs*, 2nd ed. [London: William Kimber, 1952], pp. 14-15).

25 Patriot] Cf. note 10.

26 Lines 65-68] "This is a true story, which happened in the reign of William III, to an unsuspected old Patriot, who coming out at the back-door from having been closeted by the King, where he had received a large bag of Guineas, the bursting of the bag discovered his business there" (P).

27 imp'd] Imp: "*Falconry.* To engraft feathers in a damaged wing, so as to restore or improve the powers of flight . . . To imp wings *on* or *to* a person; to imp *with* wings" (*OED*, which cites this line as an illustration).

28 Line 72] "In our author's time, many Princes had been sent about the world, and great changes of Kings projected in Europe. The partition-treaty had dispos'd of Spain; France had set up a King of England, who was sent to Scotland, and back again; King Stanislaus was sent to Poland, and back again; the Duke of Anjou was sent to Spain, and Don Carlos to Italy" (P). Pope refers to the second Partition Treaty, completed in February 1700 (N.S.) between William III and Louis XIV, according to which the Archduke Charles, second son of the Emperor Leopold, received the throne of Spain, the Spanish Netherlands, and the Spanish territorial possessions.

29 Line 74] "Alludes to several Ministers, Counsellors, and Patriots banished in our times to Siberia, and to that MORE GLORIOUS FATE of the PARLIAMENT OF PARIS, banished to Pontoise in the year 1720" (P). The Parliament of Paris was opposed to the grandiose financial maneuvers of the Scottish economist John Law (1671-1729), father of the "Mississippi scheme" (cf. note 59). The Regent, however, had full confidence in Law and banished the Parliament, as Pope says.

30 Sibyl's] The Cumæan Sibyl, who wrote her prophecies on leaves and then allowed the wind to blow them away. Cf. Vergil *Aeneid* iii. 445-452; vi. 74-76.

31 Line 78] "Queen Caroline was supposed to have received a large present from [Robert] Knight, the runaway cashier of the South Sea Company. See Pope's letter to Swift, 28th Nov., 1729 . . ." (EC). The letter in question (*Corr*, III, 80) says plainly that, so far as Pope knew, the Queen accepted the bribe; but the story was only a rumor.

32 Lines 79-80] This is the pre-1744 reading, printed here because it does not have the character of a dialogue. The 1751 edition gives the couplet as follows:

> Since then, my Lord, on such a World we fall,
> What say you? *B.* Say? Why take it, Gold and all.

These are lines 77-78 in the 1751 edition. The couplet following is also in dialogue form in the 1751 edition.

33 Line 82] EC compares Juvenal *Satires* 14. 36-38. Cf. *Im. Hor.*, Ep. ii. 2. 226-229.

34 Turner] "One, who, being possessed of three hundred thousand pounds, laid down his Coach, because Interest was reduced from five to four *per cent.* and then put seventy thousand into the Charitable Corporation [cf. note 46] for better interest; which sum having lost, he took it so much to heart, that he kept his chamber ever after. It is thought he would not have outliv'd it, but that he was heir to another considerable estate, which he daily expected, and that by this course of life he sav'd both cloaths and all other expences" (P). Richard Turner (d. 1733), known as "Plum" (cf. note 55) Turner, had been a Turkey merchant.

35 Wharton] "A Nobleman of great qualities, but as unfortunate in the application of them, as if they had been vices and follies. See his character in the first Epistle [*Ep. Cob.*, lines 178-209 and note 44]" (P).

36 Hopkins] "A Citizen, whose rapacity obtained him the name of *Vultur Hopkins.* He lived worthless, but died *worth three hundred thousand pounds*, which he would give to no person living, but left it so as not to be inherited till after the second generation. His counsel representing to him how many years it must be, before this could take effect, and that his money could only lie at interest all that time, he exprest great joy thereat, and said, 'They would then be as long in spending, as he had been in getting it.' But the Chancery afterwards set aside the will, and gave it to the heir at law" (P). The facts concerning the will of John Hopkins (1663-1732) are given incorrectly by Pope; EC and TE note the details. Cf. line 291-298 and note 95.

37 Line 88] For Chartres cf. note 6 and *Ep. Lady*, note 21.
"JAPHET CROOK, alias Sir *Peter Stranger,* was punished with the loss of those parts, for having forged a conveyance of an Estate to himself, upon which he took up several thousand pounds. He was at the same time sued in Chancery for having fraudulently obtain'd a Will by which he possess'd another considerable Estate, in wrong of the brother of the deceas'd. By these means he was *worth* a great sum, which (in reward for the small loss of his ears) he enjoy'd in prison till his death, and quietly left to his executor" (P). Crook (1662-1734) was punished thus in the pillory in 1731; cf. *Ep. Arb.*, 363; *Ep. Sat.*, I, 120; II, 185-190.

38 Hippia] "Hippia" has not been identified.

39 Fulvia] "Fulvia" has not been identified. The Roman Fulvia (d. 40 B.C.) was the first wife of Mark Antony (he was her third husband;

her first, P. Clodius Pulcher, was brother to Catullus' "Lesbia" and an enemy of Cicero). Another Fulvia was the mistress of Q. Curius, one of the Catilinarian conspirators; she divulged to Cicero Catiline's plot against his life and against the government. *Buckle*: cf. note 96.

40 Narses] In the Huntington MS the name appears variously as "Cxxxn" and "old Gen'ral" (cf. Wasserman, pp. 110-111). The reference is to William Cadogan, first Earl Cadogan (1675-1726), who rendered distinguished military service under Marlborough in the War of the Spanish Succession. He was especially famous as commanding officer of a valiant Irish regiment (Cadogan himself was of a Dublin family) popularly known as "Cadogan's Horse." He was instrumental in suppressing the Jacobite rebellion of 1715-1716 in Scotland (cf. note 28) and was created earl in 1718. Although his Jacobite enemies circulated many unpleasant rumors about Cadogan (he and Atterbury particularly disliked each other), he was a useful and energetic soldier and diplomat; among other things, he negotiated the Quadruple Alliance between England, France, Holland, and the Empire in 1718. Cf. *Ep. Burl.*, note 48.

There have been several historical persons named Narses, the most celebrated of whom is Narses the eunuch (c. A.D. 478-573), an important military officer and rival of Belisarius under Justinian. His character and exploits are described by Gibbon (*Decline and Fall of the Roman Empire*, Ch. XLIII).

41 Harpax] "Harpax" was "Sxxxk" in the Huntington MS (cf. Wasserman, pp. 80-81, 110-111), that is, Charles Douglas, Earl of Selkirk, a well-known and unpopular Scottish peer. He is the "Shylock" of line 117; cf. *Ep. Cob.*, note 17. He is also mentioned in *Ep. Sat.*, I, 92; II, 61-62.

42 Doctor] Cf. note 3.

43 Shylock] The Huntington MS reads "Worldly" (cf. Wasserman, pp. 83, 110-111), for whom see note 17; cf. also notes 41 and 51 and *Ep. Cob.*, note 17.

44 Line 98] "A famous Dutchess of R. in her last will left considerable legacies and annuities to her Cats" (P). This is Frances Theresa Stewart, Duchess of Richmond and Lennox (1647-1702). One of the most beautiful women in the kingdom, she was educated in France in the household of the Dowager Queen Henrietta Maria. When she returned to England, she broke many hearts, including that of Charles II, whose mistress she became and who nearly attempted to divorce Queen Catherine on her account. Forbidden by Charles to marry, she eloped in 1667 with her cousin Charles, third Duke of Richmond and sixth Duke of Lennox. Pope's statement about the will of "La Belle Stewart" is inaccurate.

45 Lines 99-100] Cf. *Im. Hor.*, Sat., ii. 2. 166-179.

46 Lines 101-102] "This epistle was written in the year 1730, when a corporation was established to lend money to the poor upon

pledges, by the name of the *Charitable Corporation;* but the whole was turned only to an iniquitous method of enriching particular people, to the ruin of such members, that it became a parliamentary concern to endeavour the relief of those unhappy sufferers, and three of the managers, who were members of the house, were expelled [Bond, Sir Robert Sutton, and Sir Archibald Grant]. By the report of the committee, appointed to enquire into that iniquitous affair, it appears, that when it was objected to the intended removal of the office, that the Poor, for whose use it was erected, would be hurt by it, Bond, one of the Directors, replied, Damn the Poor. That "God hates the poor," and, "That every man in want is knave or fool," &c. were the genuine apothegms of some of the persons here mentioned" (P). Denis Bond (d. 1747) was not only one of the directors of the scandalous Charitable Corporation for the Relief of the Industrious Poor but was also party to another fraud, that connected with the sale of the estates of James Radcliffe, third Earl of Derwentwater (1689-1716). Derwentwater, a Roman Catholic and a Jacobite, had joined the uprising in Scotland in 1715 and was attainted and executed the following year. According to Hervey's *Memoirs* (1884), I, 228, the trustees of the sale of the estates thus forfeited "had cheated the public of an immense sum"; and Bond was so deeply involved that he was expelled from Parliament. Cf. *Im. Hor.*, Sat. ii. I. 44; *Ep. Sat.*, I, 121.

47 Sir Gilbert] Sir Gilbert Heathcote (1651?-1733), Lord Mayor of London, was one of the founders and subsequently Governor of the Bank of England. A Whig, he was famous for his wealth, his parsimony, and his universal unpopularity. He was said to have been worth approximately £700,000 at his death. In the Huntington MS a modified version of this couplet appears in the portrait of "Cotta," after what is now line 180 (cf. Wasserman, pp. 86-87). Cf. *Im. Hor.*, Ep. ii. 2. 240; *Dunciad*, II, 251-252.

48 Blunt] Cf. line 135 and note 60.

49 the good Bishop] The pre-1744 editions give a different reading:
> But rev'rend S * * n with a softer air,
> Admits, and leaves them, Providence's care.

This is Sir Robert Sutton (1672-1746), who, according to EC, had given Warburton the living of Brand Broughton. Thus indebted, Warburton removed the allusion in 1744, or persuaded Pope to do so, and suppressed a portion of Pope's note (cf. note 46) in which Sutton is named as one of those guilty of embezzlement in the matter of the Charitable Corporation. A similar suppression took place in *Ep. Sat.*, I, 16. EC notes, following Croker, that Sutton was intended for the Church.

50 it] As EC notes, there is nothing to show that *it* refers to precious metal. Pope doubtless meant gold, but there is no grammatical antecedent for *it.*

51 Shylock] The 1732 edition (line 115) reads "S--l--k" (cf. Wasserman, p. 139). Cf. notes 41 and 43.

52 Lines 119-120] "In the extravagance and luxury of the South-sea year, the price of a haunch of Venison was from three to five pounds" (P). The South Sea Company was incorporated in 1711 as a joint-stock company to which the government was to sell trading monopolies, thereby reducing the national debt. In 1720, the company undertook, in return for further concessions, to liquidate the entire national debt. Many people, including Pope himself, bought shares; and by the summer of 1720 speculation had reached the point of mania. That autumn, however, the stock began to drop, and by the following year the inevitable crash was complete. The skill and leadership exercised by Sir Robert Walpole averted an even more serious crisis, and in 1721 the Bubble Act was passed, forbidding the formation of joint-stock companies without a royal charter. The company maintained a precarious existence until 1853, when it became defunct.

53 Lines 121-122] "Many people about the year 1733, had a conceit that such a thing was intended, of which it is not improbable this lady might have some intention" (P). It was by no means improbable, since "Phryne" is Mary Skerrit (d. 1738), Sir Robert Walpole's mistress, whom he married in 1738, a year after the death of his wife. Queen Caroline could never understand how the beautiful Miss Skerrit (or Skerrett) could love a man like Walpole "avec ce gros corps, ces jambes enflées, et ce vilain ventre" (Hervey, II, 143). Walpole's Excise Bill of 1733 created such public alarm that it had to be withdrawn. Cf. *Ep. Cob.*, note 2.

54 Sappho] Here, as usual, "Sappho" means Lady Mary Wortley Montagu (cf. *Ep. Lady*, note 10). She was a close friend of Mary Skerrit, and Pope told Spence that lines 121-124 referred to them (Spence, p. 371).

55 plum] "(In the cant of the city.) The sum of one hundred thousand pounds" (Johnson's Dictionary, which cites this line as an illustration). Cf. note 34. This passage on fear as a motive for avarice (lines 115-124) suggests *Im. Hor.*, Ep. i. 1. 67-70.

56 Peter] "PETER WALTER, a person not only eminent in the wisdom of his profession, as a dextrous attorney, but allow'd to be a good, if not a safe, conveyancer; extremely respected by the Nobility of this land, tho' free from all manner of luxury and ostentation: his Wealth was never seen, and his bounty never heard of, except to his own son, for whom he procured an employment of considerable profit, of which he gave him as much as was *necessary*. Therefore the taxing this gentleman with any ambition, is certainly a great wrong to him" (P). Cf. note 6.

57 Didius] "A Roman Lawyer, so rich as to purchase the Empire when it was set to sale upon the death of Pertinax" (P). Helvius Pertinax, emperor of Rome from January 1 to March 28, A.D. 193, succeeded Commodus as emperor. He was killed by the praetorian guards, who then put the empire up for sale at auction. Didius Salvius Julianus bought it for 6250 drachmas and assumed

the throne. Two months later he was deposed and executed by the senate and was succeeded by Septimius Severus. Cf. Gibbon, *Decline and Fall of the Roman Empire*, Ch. V.

58 Lines 129-130] Since 1573 the electoral crown of Poland had periodically been put up for grabs. Anthony Ashley Cooper (Dryden's "Achitophel") had aspired to it himself before the election of John Sobieski in 1674 (cf. Dryden, *The Medal*, lines 3 and 15, and "Epistle to the Whigs"). On February 1, 1733, the death of Augustus II left it once more open to competition; on October 5, 1733, his son, the elector of Saxony, was proclaimed Augustus III. The electors were very susceptible to bribery.

59 Lines 130-134] "The two persons here mentioned were of Quality, each of whom in the Missisippi [*sic*] despis'd to realize above *three hundred thousand pounds*; the Gentleman with a view to the purchase of the Crown of Poland, the Lady on a vision of the like royal nature. They since retired into Spain, where they are still in search of gold in the mines of the Asturias" (P). Joseph Gage, Count Gage (1678?-1753?), accumulated a vast fortune in the Mississippi colonization scheme (1712-1721) of John Law, the Scottish economist (cf. note 29). As Pope says, he attempted to purchase the crown of Poland for three million pounds, and he then offered to buy the island of Sardinia from Victor Amadeus (cf. *Ep. Cob.*, *notes* 36, 37). Both offers were refused. His second wife was Lady Mary Herbert, daughter of the second Marquis Powis. She joined Gage in the mines of Asturias, in northern Spain, after the collapse of the Mississippi scheme had ruined his fortune. Gage subsequently (1742) entered the army of Spain and was made a grandee for his military services in the War of the Austrian Succession.

60 Blunt] "SIR JOHN BLUNT, originally a scrivener, was one of the first projectors of the South-sea company, and afterwards one of the directors of the famous scheme in 1720. He was also one of those who suffer'd most severely by the bill of pains and penalties on the said directors. He was a Dissenter of a most religious deportment, and profess'd to be a great believer. Whether he did really credit the prophecy here mentioned is not certain, but it was constantly in this very style he declaimed against the corruption and luxury of the age, the partiality of Parliaments, and the misery of party-spirit. He was particularly eloquent against *Avarice* in great and noble persons, of which he had indeed liv'd to see many miserable examples. He died in the year 1732 [*sic*]" (P). Blunt (1665-1733) is mentioned in line 105 and in Pope's note to line 20 (note 6).

61 Patriot] Cf. lines 37, 65, 150; and notes 10, 25, 65.

62 Box] Pope may mean the theater box or the dice box. *Bite* (line 143): "to deceive" (*OED*, which cites line 143 as an example); Cf. note 108.

63 pack] "To sort the cards so as that the game shall be iniquitously

secured. It is applied to any iniquitous procurement of collusion"
(Johnson's Dictionary).

64 Line 146] Edward III, in 1340, was the first English monarch to
quarter the arms of France on his own to signify his claim to the
French throne. In accordance with the Treaty of Union with Scotland
in 1707, Queen Anne rearranged the royal arms and retained the three
fleurs-de-lis of France. They were not removed until 1801, when
the English claim to the throne of France was officially dropped.
Cf. Francis J. Grant, *The Manual of Heraldry*, rev. ed. (Edinburgh:
John Grant, Booksellers, Ltd., 1952), pp. 134-135.

65 Patriot] Cf. lines 37, 65, 141; and notes 10, 25, 61.

66 Line 152] EC notes that this refers to the scheme of the South
Sea Company to liquidate the whole national debt (cf. note 52).
When the plan was approved by Parliament, "men of all shades of
political opinion rushed to buy stock, [and] Blunt is said by Pope
to have bought both sides" (EC, 144).

67 Lines 155-156] For Pope's theory of the Ruling Passion, cf. *Es. Man*,
II, 123-202, and *Ep. Cob.*, lines 174 ff. Cf. also the introduction,
pp. 15-22 above.

68 Lines 157-160] Cf. *Es. Man*, II, 59-66.

69 Lines 161-164] Cf. *Es. Man*, II, 205-206:
> Extremes in Nature equal ends produce,
> In Man they join to some mysterious use.

EC notes that these passages are proof positive of the fatalism
supposedly inherent in Pope's theory of the Ruling Passion. Cf. the
introduction, pp. 18-21 and pp. 54-58 above, and *Ep. Burl.*, note 54.

70 Lines 165-170] Cf. Gen. 8:22 and Vergil *Georgics* i. 1-42.

71 Line 172] Cf. Prov. 23:5.

72 Lines 173-179] An echo of the thought in lines 13-14, and a basic
theme of the poem. Cf. *Ep. Lady*, lines 149-150 and note 36; *Im.
Hor.*, Ep. ii. 2. 245-262. EC and TE both note that the lines closely
resemble a passage in Thomas May's comedy *The Old Couple*
(1658), Act III:
> . . . some men were made to be
> The conduit-pipes of an estate, or rather
> The sieves of fortune, through whose leaking holes
> She means to scatter a large flood of wealth,
> Besprinkling many with refreshing showers.
> So usurers, so dying aldermen
> Pour out at once among their sieve-like heirs
> Whole gusts of envi'd wealth; which they together
> Through many holes let out again in showers,
> And with their ruin water a whole country.

W. Carew Hazlitt (ed.) *A Select Collection of Old English Plays
Originally Published by Robert Dodsley in the Year* 1744, 4th ed.

(London: Reeves and Turner, 1875), XII, 42. A note on the passage refers to Pope's epistle.

73 Cotta] Neither old "Cotta" nor his son can be identified with certainty. For a discussion of some possibilities, cf. TE's note; EC is silent on the subject.

74 Lines 181-182] This is a clear echo of Dryden's "Shimei" (Slingsby Bethel, the Whig sheriff of London) in *Absalom and Achitophel,* lines 620-621. Cf. note 110 and introduction, p. 59 above.

75 Line 184 "—dapibus mensas onerabat inemptis. VIRG." (P). The allusion is to Vergil *Georgics* iv. 133 Cf. the introduction, pp. 59-61 above. There is a similar praise of home-grown delicacies in Juvenal *Satires* 11. 64-89.

76 Chartreux] This is the celebrated Carthusian monastery of La Grande Chartreuse, in the mountainous country near Grenoble, France. The austere Carthusian order was founded here by Saint Bruno in the eleventh century. Cf. the introduction, p. 59 above.

77 Line 199] In Warburton's commentary on the lines the two Cottas are described as examples of the two opposite Ruling Passions which the poem has up to now been describing. Cf. *Im. Hor.*, Sat, ii. 2. 45-46.

78 Yet sure . . . raise] These two lines were found by Warburton in the MS and added by him, possibly with Pope's permission. Although they anticipate the lines which follow, they are not recognized by TE or Wasserman as representing Pope's own intentions. They are not included in the line numbering here. Warburton's note is as follows: "This, tho' a certain truth, will, as I apprehend, never make its fortune in the City: yet, for all that, the poet has fully approved his maxim in the following description."

79 hecatombs] Cf. *Ep. Burl.*, line 156 (note 52) where the word is also used to describe a lavish banquet (Timon's). A note signed SCRIBL. in the 1751 edition reads as follows: "Our author represents this, as it truly was designed, a *Sacrifice* to the Church, to render it propitious, in a time of danger, to the State." In both poems the word has ritualistic connotations.

80 House] The House of Hanover, but cf. Ps. 69:9.

81 Train-bands] "The militia; the part of a community trained to martial exercise" (Johnson's Dictionary). EC notes that the train-bands of the city of London were always Whig. OED uses this line to illustrate the word.

82 Lines 179-218] This entire passage on "Cotta" and his son is strongly reminiscent of *Im. Donne*, II, 109-124, including the references to the Carthusians and to hecatombs.

83 Lines 219-228] Cf. *Im. Hor.*, Sat. ii. 2. 45-48, 61-62; Ep ii. 2. 284-295.

84 Line 230] Cf. lines 107-108, 188.

85 Line 240] An echo of Dryden's "Zimri" (George Villiers, second Duke of Buckingham) in *Absalom and Achitophel*, line 550. Villiers enters the present poem at line 299.

86 OXFORD's] "Edward Harley, Earl of Oxford. The son of Robert, created Earl of Oxford and Earl Mortimer by Queen Anne. This Nobleman died regretted by all men of letters, great numbers of whom had experienc'd his benefits. He left behind him one of the most noble Libraries in Europe" (P). Edward Harley (1689-1741) was the son of Robert Harley, first Earl of Oxford (1661-1724), the famous statesman and founder of the Harleian collection of books and manuscripts which helped to form the nucleus of the British Museum. Cf. *Ep. Burl.*, note 7.

87 Lines 245-246] Warburton's note to this passage reads in part as follows: ". . . But the more constant these [i.e., the graces of fortune] were, the more need had He of some superior assistance to keep him in the *golden mean*: which the ancients seem'd so well apprised of, that they gave to every man *two* Guardian Angels (here alluded to) as if, without standing on either side of him, he could not possibly be kept long in the *mean* or middle: nothing therefore could be more seasonable than this pathetic prayer on so critical an occasion."

88 the MAN OF ROSS] "The person here celebrated, who with a small Estate actually performed all these good works, and whose true name was almost lost (partly by the title of the *Man of Ross* given him by way of eminence, and partly by being buried without so much as an inscription) was called Mr. John Kyrle. He died in the year 1724, aged 90, and lies interr'd in the chancel of the church of Ross in Herefordshire" (P). Cf. *Ep. Sat.*, II, 99, and see the introduction, pp. 63-67 above.

89 Vaga] The River Wye, also called *Vaga* by John Philips in *The Splendid Shilling*, line 31. Ross is on the banks of the Wye in southern Herefordshire. In the Huntington MS the Severn (line 252) is also given its Latin name, *Sabrina* (cf. Wasserman, pp. 90-91).

90 Lines 253-274] For a detailed account of Kyrle's charities, cf. EC, 150-151, and TE, 110-112.

91 Line 254] Cf. Ex. 17:6.

92 Lines 275-286] This passage Warburton turned into a dialogue by placing *B* in front of lines 275 and 283, and *P* in front of lines 279 and 285. Parts of the passage, at least, have the appearance of dialogue, but Pope originally seems to have intended an imaginary, unidentified person to comment briefly on the poet's words. Or he may have been pretending to anticipate a comment from Bathurst.

93 Line 287] "The Parish-register" (P).

94 Lines 291-298] For Hopkins, cf. line 86 and note 36. Pope is confusing Hopkins's funeral with Cutler's; cf. note 100.

95 Lines 293-296] "The poet ridicules the wretched taste of carving large perriwigs on Busto's, of which there are several vile examples in the tombs at Westminster and elsewhere" (P). Hopkins was buried not in Westminster but in Wimbledon Churchyard, Surrey, as EC and TE report.

96 Line 296] Buckle: "The state of the hair crisped and curled, by being kept long in the same state" (Johnson's Dictionary). This description (lines 293-296) may be an ironical echo of Dryden's translation of Vergil's *Aeneid*, lines 824-831.

97 Lines 289-314] "This Lord, yet more famous for his vices than his misfortunes, after having been possess'd of about 50,000 pound a year, and past thro' many of the highest posts in the kingdom, died in the year 1687, in a remote inn in Yorkshire, reduc'd to the utmost misery" (P). This, of course, is George Villiers, second Duke of Buckingham (1628-1687), the Restoration politician and wit. He was one of the authors of *The Rehearsal* (1672), and he is the "Zimri" of Dryden's *Absalom and Achitophel* (lines 544-568). Cf. note 85. Pope's account of Buckingham's death is much exaggerated.

98 Cliveden] "A delightful palace, on the banks of the Thames, built by the Duke of Buckingham" (P). Buckingham's estate at Cliveden, Buckinghamshire, was an enormous place, but it has completely disappeared long since.

99 Shrewsbury] "The Countess of Shrewsbury, a woman abandon'd to gallantries. The Earl her husband was kill'd by the Duke of Buckingham in a duel; and it has been said, that during the combat she held the Duke's horses in the habit of a page" (P). Anna Maria, wife of Francis Talbot, eleventh Earl of Shrewsbury, was the eldest daughter of Robert Brudenell, Earl of Cardigan. Her husband was wounded in 1668 in a duel with this same Buckingham, who was her lover, and died of his wounds the following March 16. The matter is described by Pepys, January 17, 1668 (N.S.).

100 Cutler] Sir John Cutler (1608?-1693), the son of a grocer, was notorious for his personal miserliness, but Pope overlooks his notable benefactions. He endowed a lectureship at Gresham College, Oxford, contributed heavily towards the reconstruction of the halls of the Grocers' Company, built an anatomical theater for the College of Physicians, and rebuilt part of Saint Margaret's Church (parish church of the Houses of Parliament), where he was buried. The Grocers' Company placed his statue and portrait in their chambers, and the College of Physicians erected a full-length statue of him outside the Cutlerian Theater. He died worth £300,000. His funeral, against his wishes, was very expensive, costing £7666 (*DNB*). Cf. note 94.

101 doctor] Cf. note 3.

102 both] Virtue and Wealth, in line 334.

103 Lines 337-338] This is the pre-1744 reading. The later version makes
the couplet more patently a dialogue:
A knotty point! to which we now proceed.
But you are tir'd—I'll tell a tale. *B.* "Agreed."

104 Lines 339-340] "The Monument, built in memory of the fire of
London, with an inscription, importing that city to have been burnt
by the Papists" (P). The Monument, which still stands just off
King William Street on Fish Street Hill, is a fluted Doric column
designed by Sir Christopher Wren, with an emblematical sculpture
on the west side executed by Caius Gabriel Cibber (1630-1700),
father of Colley Cibber (cf. *Dunciad,* I, 29-32). The Monument
is 202 feet high and is exactly that distance from the shop in
Pudding Lane where the Fire started. It was completed in 1677.
As a result of the anti-Catholic hysteria which followed the Popish
Plot, and owing in great measure to the zealous Protestantism of
Sir Patience Ward, the Lord Mayor, inscriptions were set up on the
Monument and on the house in Pudding Lane to the effect that
the Fire had been started by Papists. This was in 1681. After the
accession of James II, the inscriptions were removed, but they were
restored in 1689 in the reign of William III. They were not finally
obliterated until 1831. Cf. Charles Welch, *History of the Monument*
(London: Corporation of the City of London, 1893), pp. 25-41.

105 Balaam] Cf. Num. 22-24. All attempts to identify Balaam have
proved inconclusive, and it is probably that Balaam, like many of
Pope's other characters, is either composite or fictitious (Cf. *Im. Hor.,*
Sat. ii. 1. 4-44). The Balaam of the Old Testament, a gentile and
a seer, was traditionally regarded by New Testament writers and by
Scriptural commentators as a symbol of avarice (cf. Wasserman,
pp. 44-45), and Pope clearly regards him as a representative of
middle-class, Whig, Puritan chicanery. For the possibility that Balaam
may have been patterned after the merchant Thomas Pitt (1653-
1726), cf. TE, 118.

106 Lines 355-356] "The author has placed the scene of these shipwrecks
in Cornwall, not only from their frequency on that coast, but from
the inhumanity of the inhabitants to those to whom that misfortune
arrives: When a ship happens to be stranded there, they have been
known to bore holes in it, to prevent its getting off; to plunder,
and sometimes even to massacre the people: Nor has the Parliament
of England been yet able wholly to suppress these barbarities" (P).
EC and TE note that the practice was finally abolished through
the influence of Wesleyan preachers.

107 chirping] "To chirp . . . (which seems apparently corrupted from
cheer up) to make cheerful, as,
"To push on the *chirping* and moderate bottle.—Johnson" (Johnson's Dictionary). *OED* cites Pope's line as an illustration.

108 Lines 361-364] In these lines Pope has in mind the East India
merchant Thomas Pitt (cf. note 105), known as "Diamond Pitt."
While in India Pitt bought the famous Pitt diamond for about

£20,000; he later sold it to the Regent of France (Philip, Duke of Orleans) for a sum reported variously as £80,000 and £135,000. In the Huntington MS what is now line 364 read, "So robbd the Robber, and was rich as -x-P-t" (cf. Wasserman, pp. 68-69). On the bottom of another page of the MS Pope made the following note: "P-tt, once Governour of Fort St. George [i.e., Madras], who there became Master of a Diamond wch he afterw^ds sold to the K. of France for one hundred & twenty thous^d pounds" (Wasserman, pp. 100-101).

      bit] To bite: "To cheat; to trick; to defraud: a low phrase" (Johnson's Dictionary, which cites these lines as an illustration). Cf. line 143.

109 Lines 369-374] An interesting blend of the legends of Danaë and Faustus.

110 Line 380] Cf. Dryden's "Shimei" (*Absalom and Achitophel*, line 588), who "never broke the Sabbath but for gain." Cf. note 74.

111 Line 388] Cf. *Im. Hor.*, Ep i. 1. 110-111.

112 flaunts] The verb is used intransitively, as in *Ep. Lady*, line 252.

113 Lines 393-394] Pope refers to the fact that the House of Commons met at St. Stephen's Chapel, Westminster; Balaam, in other words, has been elected to Parliament. Pope's note compares Juvenal *Satires* 3. 3: "atque unum civem donare *Sibyllae*." Juvenal's man, disgusted with city life, has moved from Rome to Cumae, "and one more citizen the Sibyl gains." His counterpart in Samuel Johnson's *London*, having moved from London to Wales, will "Give St. David one true Briton more" (*London*, line 8).

114 Coningsby] Thomas, Earl Coningsby (1656?-1729), was a prominent Whig member of Parliament. Short tempered and irritable, he was a virulent anti-Jacobite and anti-Catholic.

115 Line 402] Cf. Job 2:9.

1 Argument] This is the Argument of the 1751 edition.

2 "The extremes of *Avarice* and *Profusion* being treated of in the foregoing Epistle; this takes up one particular branch of the latter, the *Vanity of Expence* in people of wealth and quality; and is therefore a corollary to the preceding, just as the Epistle on the *Characters of Women* is to that *of the Knowledge and Characters of Men*. It is equally remarkable for exactness of method with the rest. But the nature of the subject, which is less philosophical, makes it capable of being analised in a much narrower compass" (W).

3 BURLINGTON] For a sketch of Burlington cf. the introduction, pp. 73-75 above. Cf. also note 59.

4 Topham] "A Gentleman famous for a judicious collection of Drawings" (P). EC and TE note that Richard Topham (d. 1735) was Keeper of the Records in the Tower and had an estate near Windsor. Cf. *Im. Hor.*, i. 1. 130-131.

5 Pembroke] Thomas Herbert, eighth Earl of Pembroke (1656-1733), was president of the Royal Society (1689-1690) and a well-known political figure from the reign of James II onward. He was a man of learning and an enthusiastic collector of the objects mentioned, many of which are still to be seen at the family estate, Wilton House, Salisbury. Many of Pembroke's marbles, which are in the Upper Cloisters there, formerly belonged to Cardinal Mazarin. Pembroke's first wife, the former Margaret Sawyer (d. 1706), may be "Arcadia's Countess" in *Ep. Lady*, line 7, note 4.

6 Hearne] Thomas Hearne (1678-1735), the son of a parish clerk, rose from poverty to become one of the most famous and most cordially detested scholars of his age. A Jacobite and a Nonjuror, he held his political beliefs with the most intemperate and uncompromising zeal, to the serious detriment of his career. In 1715, upon his angry refusal to take the oaths of allegiance to the House of Hanover, he was dismissed as Under-keeper of the Bodleian Library; he was never again permitted to enter the library or use any of its resources. Although he persistently and maliciously attacked other scholars whose political beliefs differed from his, his own scholarly work was remarkably meticulous and honest. Perhaps his most enduring achievement was the printing of the first modern edition of the *Battle of Maldon*, five years before the only extant manuscript perished in the tragic fire at Ashburnham House in 1731. Since the transcript which Hearne used was lost until 1937, his edition stood alone for two centuries; and subsequent collations have shown the Hearne edition to be remarkably accurate despite Hearne's ignorance of Anglo-Saxon. See David C. Douglas, *English Scholars, 1660-1730*, 2d. ed. (London: Eyre and Spottiswoode, 1951), pp. 178-194, to which this note is indebted. Hearne is the "Wormius" of *Dunciad*, III, 185-190.

7 Mead, Sloane] "Two eminent Physicians; the one [Mead] had an excellent Library, the other [Sloane] the finest collection in Europe of natural curiosities; both men of great learning and humanity" (P). Richard Mead, M.D. (1673-1754) was one of Pope's personal

physicians (cf. *Im. Hor.*, Ep. i. 1. 51) and also attended the royal family, in whose favor he eclipsed both Garth and Sloane. He was an avid collector of books, manuscripts, coins, and art objects, with a library of some 10,000 volumes. Sir Hans Sloane (1660-1753), first physician to George II, president of the Royal Society and of the College of Physicians, was a collector of books and curiosities of the type satirized in *Dunciad*, IV, 347-394. Under his will his collections were sold to the government for £20,000 (they were worth nearly three times that) and, together with the Harleian and Cottonian libraries, formed the nucleus of the British Museum. Horace Walpole, one of the trustees of the Sloane collection, has left an amusing account of its contents (letter to Sir Horace Mann, February 14, 1753).

8 Virro] Despite various conjectures, "Virro" has not been identified. Pope's use of this very rare Roman name suggests that he may have been thinking of Juvenal's fifth satire. The disagreeable host in that poem is named Virro, and Virro's banquet has some points in common with that of "Timon" in the present epistle (lines 151-168). An historical possessor of the name was Vibidius Virro, a Roman spendthrift whom Tiberius expelled from the senate (A.D. 17). Cf. Gilbert Highet, *Juvenal the Satirist* (London: Oxford University Press, 1962), p. 262.

9 Visto] EC identifies "Visto" as Sir Robert Walpole, but the identification is doubted by TE. However, Ripley (line 18) was Walpole's builder at Houghton, following the designs of Colin Campbell; and the two couplets seem to go together. The matter is obscure.

10 Ripley] "This man was a carpenter, employed by a first Minister, who raised him to an Architect, without any genius in the art; and after some wretched proofs of his insufficiency in public Buildings, made him Comptroller of the Board of Works" (P). For Thomas Ripley (d. 1758), cf. note 9 and *Im. Hor.*, Ep. ii. 1. 185-186; *Dunciad*, III, 327.

11 Bubo] George Bubb Dodington, first Baron Melcombe (1691-1762), was born plain George Bubb, the son of an apothecary. Upon inheriting the wealth of his uncle George Dodington (or Doddington), he assumed his mother's maiden name as being somewhat more dignified than "Bubb." He was a strange mixture of wit and folly, generosity and conceit, private loyalty and public treachery. His famous Diary is a naive attempt to justify his political chicanery. The fantastic vulgarity of his taste was displayed in his huge country seat of Eastbury in Dorsetshire (designed by Vanbrugh), his suburban villa at Hammersmith (which he called "La Trappe"), and his town house in Pall Mall. He had a fondness for lavender waistcoats and slept in a bed of orange and purple beneath a canopy of peacock feathers. Pope satirizes Dodington many times: *Im. Hor.*, Ep. ii. 2. 274-275; *Ep. Arb.*, 230-250, 279-280; *Ep. Sat.*, I, 11-12, 68; *1740*, line 55.

12 Line 23] "The Earl of Burlington was then publishing the Designs of Inigo Jones, and the Antiquities of Rome by Palladio" (P). Cf. the introduction, p. 73 above.

13 Lines 25-26] Cf. *Es. Crit.*, 424.

14 Lines 25-26] EC and TE compare Dryden's *Epistle the Fifteenth, To My Honoured Kinsman, John Driden*, lines 105-106; speaking of apothecaries, Dryden writes,

> From files a random recipe they take,
> And many deaths of one prescription make.

15 Line 30] EC and TE note that this may be an allusion to Bevis Mount, near Southampton, the home of Pope's friend Charles Mordaunt, third Earl of Peterborough (1658-1735). Cf. *Im. Hor.*, Ep. i. 1. 718.

16 dog-hole] "A vile hole; a mean habitation" (Johnson's Dictionary). EC explains that the front wall is extended ("ek'd) beyond the sides in order to make the building look larger.

17 rustic] "*Arch.* Characterized by a surface artificially roughened or left rough-hewn . . ." (*OED*).

18 Venetian door] "A Door or Window, so called, from being much practised at Venice, by Palladio and others" (Pope's note reprinted from the small octavo edition of 1735 [Griffith 389]; the note is lacking in the 1751 edition). Cf. *Im. Hor.*, Sat. ii. 6. 191-192 (this section of the poem is by Pope). The line is cited by OED.

19 your brother Peer] This person has not been identified.

20 the seven] The seven sciences of the medieval curriculum: the trivium of grammar, logic, and rhetoric; the quadrivium of music, arithmetic, geometry, and astronomy.

21 Line 46] "*Inigo Jones* the celebrated Architect, and M. Le Nôtre, the designer of the best Gardens of France" (P). Inigo Jones (1573-1651), known as "the English Palladio," was official architect to Queen Anne (queen of James I) and a designer of the repairs to St. Paul's (1633). As a maker of stage settings for court masques, he collaborated and frequently quarreled with Ben Jonson; cf. line 193. André Le Nôtre (1613-1700) planned the gardens at Versailles and Fontainebleau, which were laid out in regular, formal style; cf. line 71.

22 Line 50] Cf. *Es. Crit.*, 68-69.

23 Lines 55-56] Cf. Addison's praise of variety and surprise in *Spectator* No. 412. Pope made this same comment to Spence (c. 1742) some seven years after these lines were written; cf. Spence, p. 260.

24 intending Lines] Lines of perspective. Pope discussed with Spence (c. 1738-1739) the use of perspective and painterly techniques of landscape gardening; cf. Spence, pp. 209-210.

25 Line 66] In May 1730 Pope had remarked to Spence, "No judging of a piece fro yᵉ Scatter'd parts; yᵉ dots, & Hieroglyphic: (not as to yᵉ Great Beauty: but we may see particular beauties in yᵉ parts? That's very true" (quoted by Sherburn, "Pope at Work," *Essays on*

the Eighteenth Century Presented to David Nichol Smith, p. 51).
Cf. introduction, pp. 79-81 above, especially Warburton's comment.

26 STOW] "The seat and gardens of the Lord Viscount Cobham in Buckinghamshire" (P). This is the Cobham addressed in the first epistle. Cf. note 28 and *Ep. Cob.*, note 2. Cobham's great estate at Stowe was originally an abbey and came into the hands of Cobham's family, the Temples, in the sixteenth century. The eighteenth-century architect was Vanbrugh; and the gardens, in Pope's day the most famous in all England, were by Charles Bridgeman. Stowe is now a boys' school.

27 Nero's Terraces] Pope refers, according to EC, to the stupendous Golden House of Nero as described in Suetonius' life of that emperor, chapter 31.

28 Line 74] "An high compliment to the noble person on whom it is bestowed, as making him the *substitute of Good Sense.*—This office, in the original plan of the poem, was given to another Man of TASTE; who not having the SENSE to see a compliment was intended him convinced the poet it did not belong to him" (W). The other man of taste was Charles Bridgeman (d. 1738), a professional landscape gardener whose work Pope much admired. Bridgeman laid out the gardens at Stowe (cf. note 26) and the royal gardens at Kensington Palace and Richmond. He is thought to be the landscape gardener portrayed by Hogarth in Plate II of *The Rake's Progress*, standing just at the young heir's right and holding out a garden plan.
   Lines 75-76] "This was done in Hertfordshire, by a wealthy citizen, at the expence of above 5000 l. by which means (merely to overlook a dead plain) he let in the north-wind upon his house and parterre, which were before adorned and defended by beautiful woods" (P).

29 Line 78] "Dr. S. Clarke's busto placed by the Queen in the Hermitage, while the Dr. duely frequented the Court" (P). The Hermitage and Merlin's Cave were two ornamental and highly grotesque buildings erected by Queen Caroline in the gardens at Richmond during the 1730's. In the former Her Majesty had placed the busts of Locke, Newton, Wollaston, Boyle, and her favorite philosopher Samuel Clarke (1675-1729). Clarke's book *The Scripture Doctrine of the Trinity* (1712) was denounced as Arian; and he was once described as the most learned and honest man in the kingdom—except that he was not a Christian; cf. Basil Willey, *The Eighteenth Century Background* (London: Chatto and Windus, 1957), p. 60. For a comment on Clarke's philosophy, cf. *Dunciad*, IV, 471-472.

30 Villario] Villario has not been satisfactorily identified. EC and TE summarize the prevailing conjectures.

31 Line 80] Quincunx: "A disposition of five objects so placed that four occupy the corners, and the fifth the center of a square or rectangle" (OED). In this instance the objects so disposed are trees; cf. *Im. Hor.*, Sat. ii. 1. 129-130. Espalier: "A kind of framework of stakes upon which fruit trees or shrubs are trained . . . A fruit tree or row of trees so trained" (OED); cf. *Im. Hor.*, Sat. ii. 2. 147.

32 Line 81] Warburton's note explains this statement and reads in part as follows: "To understand what is meant by *supporting* (which is a term of art common both to *Planting* and *Painting*) we must consider what things make the natural defect or weakness of a rude uncultivated *Plain*; and these are, the having a disagreeable *flatness*, and the not having a *proper termination*. But a *Wood*, rightly disposed, takes away the one, and gives what is wanting of the other."

33 Line 84] This line is taken word for word from Pope's youthful "Cowley. The Garden" (*Imitations of English Poets*, IV), line 8.

34 Lines 87-88] Villario's inconsistency may be likened to that of Papillia, *Ep. Lady*, lines 37-40 and note 13.

35 Sabinus] This person has not been identified.

36 Line 95] "The two extremes in parterres, which are equally faulty; a *boundless Green*, large and naked as a field, or a *flourish'd Carpet*, where the greatness and nobleness of the piece is lessened by being divided into too many parts, with scroll'd works and beds, of which the examples are frequent" (P).

37 Line 96] "Touches upon the ill taste of those who are so fond of Ever-greens (particularly Yews, which are the most tonsile) as to destroy the nobler Forest-trees, to make way for such little ornaments as Pyramids of dark green continually repeated, not unlike a Funeral procession" (P). Cf. Pope, *Guardian* No. 173, and Addison, *Spectator* No. 414.

38 Line 99] "This description is intended to comprize the principles of a false Taste of Magnificence, and to exemplify what was said before, that nothing but Good Sense can attain it" (P). Pope was much embarrassed by the malicious identification of "Timon" with James Brydges, first Duke of Chandos (1673-1744), whose pretentious estate, Cannons, bore some resemblance to Timon's villa. The identification was made even more vexing by the circulation of an unfounded charge that Pope had earlier accepted a present of £1000 from Chandos. These errors persisted until the present century, when Pope was decisively vindicated in an article by the late George Sherburn, "'Timon's Villa' and Cannons," *Huntington Library Bulletin*, VIII (October, 1935), 131-170. It is now virtually certain that "Timon" is a composite figure. For an account of the discrepancies between Timon's villa and Cannons see Sherburn's article and TE, 142-147. Sherburn reprints much of the contemporary correspondence in the case. An appendix to TE (Appendix B, pp. 164-168) discusses the problem in detail. Pope's reply to these charges is set forth in *A Master Key to Popery*, a prose satire, unpublished in Pope's lifetime, directed at his accusers; it was reprinted for the first time by John Butt, *Pope and His Contemporaries*: *Essays Presented to George Sherburn*, ed. James L. Clifford and Louis A. Landa (Oxford: The Clarendon Press, 1949), pp. 45-57. It is reprinted in TE as Appendix C. Cf. *Ep. Arb.*, 300, 375; *Im. Hor.*, Sat. i. 6. 85-86; ii. 1. 41-42. See the introduction, pp. 39-40 above.

175

39 Line 110] In *A Master Key to Popery* (cf. note 38) Pope quotes a comment by Charles Talbot, Duke of Shrewsbury, on Blenheim Castle: "a Quarry of Stone above-ground" (Butt, 56).

40 Lines 117-118] On these lines Warburton has a farfetched but rather interesting note: "This is exactly the *two puddings* of the citizen in the foregoing fable [*Ep. Bath.*, lines 359-360], only served up a little more magnificently: But both on the same absurd principle of wrong taste, viz. that one can never have too much of a good thing."

41 Amphitrite] The fact that Amphitrite was a Nereid, wife of Poseidon, emphasizes the incongruity of line 125.

42 Line 124] "The two statues of the *Gladiator pugnans* and *Gladiator moriens*" (P).

43 Nilus] The Roman name for the Nile. The esthetic principles of landscape gardening enunciated in this poem show Pope to have been something of an authority on the subject, and the influence of Pope on eighteenth-century gardening tastes has been recognized. Cf. Sherburn, " 'Timon's Villa' and Cannons," p. 152.

44 Lines 135-140] "The false Taste in Books; a satire on the vanity in collecting them, more frequent in men of Fortune than the study to understand them. Many delight chiefly in the elegance of the print, or of the binding; some have carried it so far, as to cause the upper shelves to be filled with painted books of wood; others pique themselves so much upon books in a language they do not understand, as to exclude the most useful in one they do" (P). Cf. Leonora's library in *Spectator* No. 37.

45 Line 136] Aldus Manutius (Aldo Manuzio, born Teobaldo Mannucci, 1450-1515), was the famous Italian printer who founded the Aldine Press at Venice about 1490. Augustin Dusëuil (1673-1746) was a Parisian bookbinder who worked for the Duchess of Berry (1714) and for Louis XV (1717).

46 Lines 141-144] "The false Taste in *Music*, improper to the subjects, as of light airs in churches, often practised by the organists, &c" (P). The totally inappropriate music played in Timon's chapel doubtless took its character from the frivolous style of the Italian operas of the day; cf. *Dunciad*, IV, 57-62. Quirk: "Loose light Tune" (Johnson's Dictionary, which cites lines 141-143 as an illustration).

47 Line 145] "—And in *Painting* (from which even Italy is not free) of naked figures in Churches, &c. which has obliged some Popes to put draperies on some of those of the best masters" (P).

48 Line 146] "Verrio (Antonio) painted many cielings [*sic*], &c. at Windsor, Hampton-court, &c. and Laguerre at Blenheim-castle, and other places" (P). Antonio Verrio (1639-1707) was born at Lecce, near Otranto. Invited to England by Charles II, he did much of the decorating at Windsor Castle. In the reign of William III he painted the great staircase at Hampton Court, where he died June 17, 1707. Louis Laguerre (1663-1721), a godson of Louis XIV, was

employed for a time by Verrio in England. He did paintings at St. Bartholomew's Hospital and at Hampton Court. His portrait of William, first Earl Cadogan (the "Narses" of *Ep. Bath.*, lines 91-92), hangs in the National Portrait Gallery.

49 Lines 149-150)] "This is a fact; a reverend Dean preaching at Court, threatened the sinner with punishment in 'a place which he thought it not decent to name in so polite an assembly' " (P). TE identifies the dean as Knightly Chetwood (1650-1720), Dean of Gloucester, chaplain to James II. Cf. *Ep. Arb.*, 299-300.

50 Line 153] "Taxes the incongruity of *Ornaments* (tho' sometimes practised by the ancients) where an open mouth ejects the water into a fountain, or where the shocking images of serpents, &c. are introduc'd in Grotto's or Buffets" (P). This, too, is part of Pope's attack on baroque tastes; the fountains at the Villa d'Este, for example, are famous for such things.

51 Lines 155-164] "The proud Festivals of some men are here set forth to ridicule, where pride destroys the ease, and formal regularity all the pleasurable enjoyment of the entertainment" (P). Pope's views on the pleasures of dining are also presented in *Im. Hor.*, Sat. ii. 2. 1-8.

52 Hecatomb] The same word, in the same excessively ritualistic sense, is used of young Cotta's banquets, *Ep. Bath.*, line 203, note 79.

53 Line 160] "See Don Quixote, chap. xlvii" (P). Pope is referring to Part II of Cervantes' novel.

54 Lines 169-172] "The *Moral* of the whole, where PROVIDENCE is justified in giving Wealth to those who squander it in this manner. A bad Taste employs more hands, and diffuses Expence more than a good one. This recurs to what is laid down in Book i. [i.e., the *Essay on Man*] Epist. II. v 230-7, and in the Epistle preceding this, v 161 [163], &c" (P). Cf. *Ep. Bath.*, note 69.

55 Lines 173-176] Cf. *Im. Hor.*, Ep. ii. 2. 256-263. Ceres (line 176) is the Roman goddess of agriculture, equivalent to the Greek Demeter. The ancient legends associated with this goddess make it clear that her absence was associated with winter, or death, and her reappearance with spring, or rebirth. "Had the Poet lived but three Years longer, he had seen this prophecy fulfulled" (W). This note of Warburton's suggests that he, too, believed that "Timon" was Chandos and the villa Cannons. Both Pope and Chandos died in 1744, and Cannons was demolished in 1747.

56 Line 178] The recipients, respectively, of *Ep. Bath.* and the present epistle.

57 Lines 185-186] The language of this couplet suggests the opening lines of Dryden's *The Hind and the Panther.*

58 Line 191] Cf. *Dunciad*, III, 327-328.

59 Line 193] For Jones, cf. note 21. For Burlington's connection with Palladio, cf. introduction, pp. 73-75 above.

60 Vitruvius] M. Vitruvius Pollio (born c. 88 B.C.), a military engineer in Julius Caesar's African army (c. 50-26 B.C.), was in his old age the author of a treatise on architecture in ten books, *De Architectura* (c. 27 B.C.). He was concerned with water supply and materials and methods of construction, as well as with style.

61 Lines 195-204] "The poet after having touched upon the proper objects of Magnificence and Expence, in the private works of great men, comes to those great and public works which become a prince . . ." (P). The note goes on to detail at some length the need for such public works as bridges, dams, and roads; cf. TE, 150-151.

62 Line 204] EC and TE compare Dryden's translation of Vergil's *Aeneid* vi. 852 ("hae tibi erunt artes"): "These are imperial arts, and worthy thee."

NOTES

NOTES